Standing Up to the **MADNESS** . .

Keep

Democracy Now!

Standing Up

HYPERION New York

to the **MADNESS**

ORDINARY HEROES IN EXTRAORDINARY TIMES

AMY GOODMAN

AND

DAVID GOODMAN

Library of Congress Cataloging-in-Publication Data has been applied for.

ISBN-13: 978-1-4013-2288-5

Hyperion Books are available for special promotions, premiums, or corporate training. For details contact Michael Rentas, Proprietary Markets, Hyperion, 77 West 66th Street, 12th floor, New York, New York 10023, or call 212-456-0133.

Design by Fritz Metsch
First Edition
10   9   8   7   6   5   4   3   2   1

To our extraordinary mother,
Dorrie Goodman,
Our hero

Contents

Acknowledgments

Our deepest thanks go to the courageous people whose struggles are the subject of this book. In particular, Malik Rahim, Raed Jarrar, Peter Chase, Janet Nocek, George Christian, Jean Maria Arrigo, Steven Reisner, Stephen Soldz, Bonnie Dickinson and the student cast members of *Voices in Conflict,* Caseptla Bailey, Robert Bailey, Theo Shaw, Tina Jones, Augustín Aguayo, Ehren Watada, Liam Madden, and Jonathan Hutto were especially generous with their time, and trusted us to tell their stories well. We hope we have done them justice.

We are also grateful to the folks at Hyperion who encouraged us to share these stories. Thanks to editors Leslie Wells and Zareen Jaffery; to Christine Ragasa for getting out the word; and to Will Schwalbe and Bob Miller for having faith.

Thanks as always to our agent Luke Janklow for the magic he works, and to Claire Dippel. And thanks to Anthony Arnove for helping to get our words out across the pond.

We are grateful to those who helped us in our travels and

with our ideas. Thanks to *Democracy Now!* producer Mike Burke for help with book research. Thanks also to Jacquie Soohen and Rick Rowley of Big Noise Films for their invaluable help in Louisiana. A heartfelt thanks to Denis Moynihan for the intelligence and humanity that he brings to everything he does.

Our hats are off to the remarkable team of producers who bring *Democracy Now!* to the world every day, including Sharif Abdel Kouddous, Anjali Kamat, Jeffrey Hagerman, Robby Karran, Steve Martinez, Aaron Maté, and Nicole Salazar. With their ears tuned to the streets, to the resisters and to the activists, this amazing group of people breaks news that makes a difference, and breaks the silence imposed by the ever-consolidating corporate media. And there would be no *Democracy Now!* (or later) without Juan Gonzalez, Karen Ranucci, Julie Crosby, Emily Calhoun, Mike Castleman, Samantha Chamblee, Andres Conteris, Michael Di Filippo, Hugh Gran, Clara Ibarra, Angie Karran, Michael Kimber, Peter Kurys, Hany Massoud, Emma Missouri, Brenda Murad, Miguel Nogueira, Edith Penty, Isis Phillips, Dave Rice, Jeremy Scahill, Chuck Scurich, Silky Shah, Neil Shibata, Rebecca Silver, Becca Staley, Joy Hornung, and Jim Carlson.

Thanks also to Patrick Lannan, Andy Tuch, Laurie Betlach, Randall Wallace, Brenda Coughlin, Diana Cohn, Israel Taub, Irma Weiss, Jon Alpert, and Keiko Tsuno. And thanks to Caren Spruch, Elisabeth Benjamin, Dan Coughlin, and Maria Carrion.

From David: Hugs and thanks to Ariel and Jasper, who allow me time away to research and write, and are the two biggest reasons I always come back. And to Sue Minter, the love of my life, who makes the world—and my world—better every day.

From both of us: Thanks to our family, Dan Goodman, Yu-jin Weng, Steve Goodman, Ruth Levine, and Anna, Sarah, and Eli. As always, the memory of our late father, George Goodman, continues to inspire and guide us. Finally, a heartfelt thanks to our mother, Dorrie Goodman, to whom we dedicate this book. No writers could have a better editor and cheerleader. And no son and daughter could wish for a wiser and more loving mom.

Standing Up to the **MADNESS**

First they ignore you. Then they laugh at you. Next they fight you. Then you win.

—attributed to Mohandas K. Gandhi

Introduction

"We Will Not Be Silent"

"When fascism comes to America it will be wrapped in the American flag."

This prophetic warning, variously attributed to author Sinclair Lewis and Louisiana governor Huey Long, could have been written about post-9/11 America. Using fear, electoral fraud, and the smokescreen of terrorist attacks, the Bush administration has given us a lesson in how quickly a nation can be hijacked and core tenets of democracy trampled. Who would have imagined that once sacred principles of liberty—the right to a fair and timely trial, the checks and balances that keep our political leaders from being dictators, the freedom from arbitrary detention, the international prohibitions against torture and wars of aggression—could be thrown on the scrap heap so quickly?

President George W. Bush and Vice President Dick Cheney have asserted the president's right to wield virtually unchecked power. They have used the tragedy of 9/11 to implement a radical political agenda, attempting to ram through a right-wing wish list, from gutting social security to delivering tax cuts to the rich, to discarding basic civil liberties. Our government now routinely invades the privacy of its own citizens, then pulls the cloak of national security over its operations to hide its deceptions and blunders from public view. The economy has been trashed, inequality is now at levels not seen since the Great Depression, and at least 5 million more Americans live in poverty than did at the start of the Bush presidency. Many eminent historians and economists are concluding that George W. Bush has earned the distinction of being the "worst president ever."

Where is the outrage? The U.S. corporate media and the Democrats complain politely, and then resume their deferential posture to enable the next disaster. The media, so helpful in launching the Iraq War by acting as a conveyor belt for Bush administration lies, has shifted targets and now passes along White House propaganda about Iran.

As for the so-called opposition party that assumed control of Congress following their electoral landslide in November 2006, Democrats have boldly flexed their muscle . . . by rubber-stamping Bush's war on the Constitution. In a series of remarkable capitulations in late 2007, the Democratic majority in Congress approved President Bush's request for expanded warrantless wiretapping of Americans, once again cowed by White House propaganda about being "soft on terrorism"; approved hundreds of billions of dollars in Iraq War funding requests by President Bush; embraced retired Lt. Gen. Ricardo Sanchez by having him deliver the Democratic response to President Bush's weekly address, in spite of the fact that Sanchez has been accused in at least three lawsuits of having authorized the torture of prisoners at Abu Ghraib prison; and approved the nomination of Attorney General Michael Mukasey, despite his refusal to acknowledge that waterboarding prisoners is torture. And in 2002 and 2003, top Democrats, including current House Speaker Nancy Pelosi, raised almost no formal objections to torture techniques, including waterboarding, after being briefed on it by the CIA.[1]

It is business as usual in our one-party state.

The damage to our society that has resulted from the actions and inactions of our political leaders runs deep. Some of the damage can be quantified: thousands of American soldiers killed in a war of choice in Iraq, tens of thousands wounded and maimed, and untold numbers of servicemen and women discarded by their own government and condemned to a lifetime struggling with post-traumatic stress disorder. More than a million Iraqis killed in a pointless and hopeless war and occupation. A great American city destroyed first by Hurricane Katrina, then ravaged by racism and official neglect. Thousands of immigrants rounded up in midnight raids and deported. The list goes on and on.

Then there is the psychic damage done to our society. When the president and vice president champion the use of warrantless spying, detention without trial, and torture as valuable tools for dealing with "enemies" (which is anyone whom the president so designates), these once reviled practices suddenly become normal. Torture is now an everyday occurrence in the United States. Witness the almost casual use of Taser stun guns, which the UN has deemed to be a form of torture. Bystander videos are routinely posted on YouTube and other Web sites of innocent people being Tasered: In September 2007, police Tasered and arrested 21-year-old journalism major Andrew Meyer at a lecture given by Sen. John Kerry at the University of Florida after the student tried to question Kerry about African-American disenfranchisement in the 2004 presidential elections; a young couple in Brattle-boro, Vermont, were Tasered by police while chained to a bar-rel during a peaceful protest against the construction of a truck stop on a vacant lot in July 2007; UCLA police repeat-edly shocked an Iranian-American student with a Taser in November 2006 when he failed to show a student ID as he was using the campus computer lab; and a Utah Highway Pa-trol officer Tasered a man in September 2007 for refusing to sign a speeding ticket.

Spying has also become routine. In September 2007, the New England Patriots were caught spying on the New York Jets by surreptitiously videotaping signals of the Jets coach from the sideline. Marital disputes now often involve sophis-ticated electronic eavesdropping and keystroke-tracking software that captures everything that is typed or viewed on a computer. Employees now assume that their e-mail is mon-itored by their bosses. And suspicious parents can track the movement of their children through the use of global posi-tioning systems in cell phones.

The United States has now become an "endemic surveil-lance society," according to a report by Privacy International and the Electronic Privacy Information Center. The groups now rank the United States as the worst country in the demo-cratic world for privacy protections.

As the nation's leaders have abdicated leadership, it has fallen to unlikely heroes to step forward and pick up the fallen torch of democracy. We have traveled the country to profile some of the movers and movements who are defend-ing the core values of America.

We met librarians in Connecticut who fought off the PATRIOT Act. Community activists in New Orleans who are rebuilding their abandoned communities in the wake of Hurricane Katrina. Psychologists fighting torture. African-American students and parents fighting racism in Louisiana. Scientists fighting global warming. And soldiers fighting for peace.

These are just some of the grassroots activists who are taking politics out of the hands of politicians and changing the course of the United States. As the Bush administration has waged war abroad and at home, it has catalyzed a vast groundswell of political action. Like rivers converging into an ocean, these movements from across the country and the political spectrum have united and are swamping the traditional bastions of power.

Bush triggered this political tsunami. Now Republicans and Democrats alike must reckon with the power of this grassroots uprising that is wresting control of our country back from the corporate profiteers, ideologues, and religious zealots. Newly minted and mobilized activists and movements have helped to counter the current regime and will have a major impact on future elections.

Great change begins with small steps taken at home. This book chronicles and celebrates the actions and visions of America's real movers and shakers—the people who have defended democracy in the face of an intense assault. We have sought out these heroes in schools, military bases, homes, and neighborhoods. We hope that by highlighting some of the grassroots activism going on around North America, readers will see themselves and their communities in these stories.

We have also included "Turning Points"—brief looks back at some of history's most creative and powerful acts of resistance. What often began as small local protests that were ridiculed and dismissed by those in power ultimately inspired and catalyzed millions, and changed the world.

Taken together, these stories of resistance reveal a new alignment of power. Rather than dividing us, the Bush administration has united people—against it and against all those who would trample hard-won liberties in pursuit of their own power and profit. The stories of struggle in this book illuminate and dignify the brave efforts taken by ordinary citizens and soldiers to defend their communities and their nation. It is a story of modern day People Power. These activists are role models for others concerned about the fate of our world.

In 1942, a group of students and their professor at the University of Munich in Germany responded to the tyranny and oppression of the Nazi regime by secretly publishing and distributing a series of six leaflets. This nonviolent resistance group called itself the White Rose. Its leaders included Hans and Sophie Scholl, a brother and sister who were devout Christians, and philosophy professor Kurt Huber. The students typed the leaflets, ran off copies, and secretly sent them by courier to cities around Nazi Germany to be left in public places. They wanted to ensure that Germans could never say that they didn't know what was happening in their name. And they hoped to inspire their fellow citizens to rise up and actively oppose the Nazi regime.

Hans and Sophie Scholl and Kurt Huber were caught by the Gestapo while distributing their sixth leaflet. They were tried for political crimes in the *Volksgerichtshof,* the so-called People's Court, and beheaded. Today, numerous buildings and streets in Germany are named for the Scholls and Huber.

Polls show that they are considered to be among the most admired people in all of German history.

As their fourth leaflet implored:

We will not be silent. We are your guilty conscience. The White Rose will not leave you in peace!

As you will read in the stories that follow, the spirit of the White Rose is alive and well.

I. *Standing Up to the* **MADNESS**

Standing Up to the Madness in 1955:
The Montgomery Bus Boycott

On Thursday, December 1, 1955, Rosa Parks, an African-American seamstress, refused to give up her seat to a white man on a city bus in Montgomery, Alabama. Blacks constituted 70 percent of the riders on the Montgomery buses, but they were required to sit in the back of the bus and give up their seats to white passengers.

"Why don't you stand up?" the bus driver demanded of Parks.

"I don't think I should have to stand up," she replied. When he threatened to call the police, she said simply, "You may do that."

Parks was promptly arrested for violating segregation laws. That night, her friend Jo Ann Robinson, a teacher and civil rights activist and member of the Women's Political Council, mimeographed thirty-five thousand fliers calling on black citizens to boycott the city's segregated buses on Monday, December 5. She and other activists passed out the handbills to students leaving school and to local civil rights leaders and clergymen. The boycott call was repeated at Sunday church services.

On December 5, 1955, 90 percent of Montgomery's black citizens stayed off the buses. That evening, black community leaders formed the Montgomery Improvement Association and selected as its leader a new pastor who had recently arrived from Boston, the Reverend Martin Luther King, Jr. The association decided to continue the boycott until key demands were met: They insisted on courteous treatment by bus operators, first-come, first-served seating, and the hiring of African-American bus drivers.

The Montgomery Bus Boycott was to last for more than a year. Some fifty thousand African-Americans carpooled, used church vehicles, rode black taxis, and walked to work. The boycott crippled white businesses and the public transit system. Meanwhile, Rosa Parks mounted a legal challenge to segregation on public transportation. The U.S. Supreme Court ultimately ruled in June 1956 that segregation in buses was unconstitutional. Parks's action was the spark that ignited the modern civil rights movement.

When Rosa Parks died in October 2005, she was described in the corporate media as a simple seamstress—"no troublemaker"—who was just too tired to give up her seat on a segregated public bus. But the media got it wrong.

The truth was that Rosa Parks was an activist who, by experience, training, and choice, was a first-class troublemaker. She grew out of movement activism and came to be a powerful inspiration to that movement.

Rosa Parks and her husband, Raymond, were both members of the National Association for the Advancement of Colored People (NAACP). Raymond Parks raised money to help in the defense of the Scottsboro Boys, a group of nine black teenagers who were falsely accused and convicted of raping two white women in Alabama in 1931. In the early 1940s, Rosa Parks became the secretary of the Montgomery NAACP chapter that was headed by E. D. Nixon, a veteran civil rights campaigner who was also president of the local branch of the Pullman Porters Union. She worked as a housekeeper and seamstress for the family of Clifford Durr, a well-known white liberal attorney. Durr and his wife, Virginia, encouraged and sponsored Parks to attend the Highlander Folk School in Tennessee, a leadership training and education center for workers' rights and racial equality.

By the early 1950s, E. D. Nixon and the NAACP were eager to challenge bus segregation. Nixon was looking for a plaintiff to champion the desegregation case. He wanted someone with strong roots in the civil rights movement and who had impeccable standing in the community. He finally asked the NAACP secretary, Rosa Parks, who reluctantly consented.

As the legendary broadcaster, author, and activist Studs Terkel told Democracy Now! in 2007, "Rosa Parks did not come out of a vacuum." Noting her history of activism and her associations with organizers and movements, Terkel insisted, "All this played a role in her one day refusing to stand up. It was never one person—remember that. It's a combination of many people, many forces."

Rosa Parks and the movement she catalyzed challenged the hated Jim Crow segregation laws and won. The brave act of this seamstress inspired freedom fighters around the world. Nelson Mandela met her shortly after his release from a South African prison after twenty-eight years. "You sustained me while I was in prison all those years," he told her.

Parks wrote in her autobiography, "People always say that I didn't give up my seat because I was tired, but that isn't true. I was not tired physically, or no more tired than I usually was at the end of a working day. I was not old, although some people have an image of me as being old then. I was forty-two. No, the only tired I was, was tired of giving in."

Chapter 1

Reclaiming Common Ground

And we know this place.
Reclaim the crown.
Hold onto the prize,
never put it down.
Be firm in the stance,
no break, no bow,
got to forward on, Mama,
make your move now.
Forward on, Baba,
make your move now.
Forward, dear children,
'cuz freedom is now.

—New Orleans Poet Sunni Patterson[1]

Malik Rahim, a barrel-chested 59-year-old man with long gray dreadlocks that arc down his back and chest, stands on a street corner in what remains of the once vibrant African-American New Orleans neighborhood known as the Lower Ninth Ward. A veteran community organizer and the former defense minister of the New Orleans chapter of the Black Panther Party in the early 1970s, Rahim has thrown his share of punches and survived many battles, as well as time in jail. All of which has been good training for the epic struggle he is now engaged in: fighting for the right of poor and working-class residents of New Orleans to return home after being uprooted by Hurricane Katrina in August 2005.

We arrived in New Orleans on the second anniversary of the hurricane. President Bush had also come on this day to applaud the revival of New Orleans. But that revival skirted the places where poor people live. "The city didn't do *nuthin'* to save this," says Malik in disgust, waving a burly arm over the devastated landscape of the Lower Ninth Ward.

Hurricane Katrina, the costliest and one of the deadliest hurricanes in American history, was not just a natural disaster. The catastrophe began with water, wind, and flooding on August 29, 2005. Today, the disaster continues for the poor and working-class people of New Orleans as they contend with "another hurricane called racism, greed, and corruption," says Malik.

When the long-forecasted hurricane drowned a great American city, the richest country in the world simply abandoned its poorest residents. President George W. Bush took in the show from his ranchette in Texas, then flew to California for a chuckling photo op with a country singer. "Heckuva job, Brownie" was the back-slapping praise he dished for his inept director of the Federal Emergency Management Agency, who didn't even realize that thousands of flood survivors were huddled, terrified and starving, downtown in the Morial Convention Center. As the hurricane roared through the Gulf states, Vice President Dick Cheney swung into action to ensure that oil pipelines came before people: Cheney's office ordered a Mississippi town to immediately restore electricity to the Colonial Pipeline Co., a company that pumps gasoline and diesel from Texas and the Gulf Coast to the Northeast. The repair delayed efforts to restore power to two rural hospitals and a number of water systems in Mississippi.[2] It was a telling indicator of the White House's priorities in the Gulf.

Two shameful weeks later, the president touched down in the darkened flooded city that was temporarily illuminated to serve as a backdrop for his speech. "Throughout the area hit by the hurricane, we will do what it takes, we will stay as long as it takes, to help citizens rebuild their communities and their lives," pledged the president. "We want evacuees to come home, for the best reasons—because they have a real chance at a better life in a place they love." Then New Orleans was plunged back into darkness—one that endures in countless ways for tens of thousands of its residents.

The Lower Ninth Ward was home to about fourteen thousand people before Hurricane Katrina, nearly all of them African-American. The former cypress swamp was settled in the mid-1800s by freed slaves and has a long history of political activism; in 1960, the all-white schools bordering the Lower Ninth became the first in the Deep South to open their doors to blacks.[3] Malik offers to show us around the neighborhood—what's left of it. He estimates that fewer than five hundred residents have returned to the Lower Ninth.

It looks as if a marauding army has swept through. Neat, orderly blocks divide up the low-lying flat plain, but there are few houses still standing, and even fewer people. We peer out on block after block of barren, overgrown lots. The detritus of life is strewn about: a stairway to nowhere here, a car

buried in debris there. Mali.
Baptist Church, one of three
munity. Where once hundreds
Sunday, weeds now lick the sides
A snare drum stands in the main ais.
drumroll. Pews caked in a quarter-inch
orderly rows facing the pulpit, as if patie.
preacher to begin his homily. Outside, a
seven feet high still rings the building.

"With all the churches in America, why c   .t some
church adopt this one?" asks Malik, stepping through the
church's shattered front door. "Where's the Christian love?"

Across the street, the Alfred Lawless High School sits de-
void of students or sounds. During Hurricane Katrina, some
4,500 people sought shelter here. The brick exterior of the
building is intact. In another blow to the community, the entire complex is now slated for demolition. It is uncertain
whether the school will be replaced.

We drive on. In a bizarre move, the city has taken great
care to mow and maintain the grass median strips in the
roads. But the places where people once lived have been left to
grow over with swamp grass. We see a few houses in various
states of gutting and reconstruction. But mostly, houses just
sit empty.

"How much rebuilding do you see here?" bellows Malik,
like an impassioned preacher. "How many hammers do you
hear? Two years later, do you hear *any* activity?"

What effort there has been in this historic neighborhood
has gone to wiping it out. In 2007, New Orleans Mayor Ray
Nagin instituted an Imminent Health Threat Demolition or-
dinance that gives residents just thirty days' notice that their

molition. To the tens of thousands of ...attered across the country, the city's meager ...tter sent to the last known address (often the ...y home), a sticker attached to the property, mentions on a city Web site and in the *Times-Picayune* newspaper—is clearly inadequate. Heaping salt on the wounds, liens are placed on properties for the cost of the demolition, setting the stage for the displaced owners not only to lose their houses, but to have to forfeit their property to the city.

The hurricane displaced people. Now the government is erasing their past and preempting their futures, one demolition at a time.

"People been here over one hundred years. Then some outsider come in and say they don't matter. The city coulda come up with tractors and maintained this place. They spent more on demolishing houses than maintaining the area," fumes Rahim.

At one point during our walk around the ghostly empty neighborhood, a military Humvee drives through tall grass, and two camo-clad young Louisiana National Guardsmen jump out. They explain that they work with New Orleans police to patrol this area. The two of them had recently served tours in Iraq. Now they are on to their next battle-front—the African-American neighborhoods of New Orleans. Malik avoids eye contact with the white soldiers as they tell us that the Louisiana National Guard—nearly half of which was in Iraq during the hurricane—was originally brought in to stop the violence following Katrina. They claim flood refugees tried to hijack evacuation buses just to go to McDonald's.

"That's a bunch of *bull*shit," spits Malik as we walk away a few minutes later. He says it is one of many racist myths about how black people ran amok after the storm. "As for us being more violence prone—who's more violent than the military?"

Malik then shows us to a corner of the Lower Ninth Ward abuzz with life. A few houses are busily being rebuilt. A sign in front of the houses declares, "Roots run deep here." A small home sits alongside a white shed with a blue tarp for a roof. Inside are racks of used clothing, as well as tools that local residents can borrow for free to renovate their homes. Strains of Charlie Parker and Miles Davis waft out of the open-air shed into the languid bayou.

Other signs dot the front yard: "We're keeping our neighborhood." "You can be involved!" And one for the sightseers who cruise by each day: "Tourist Shame on You Driving By Without Stopping and Paying to See My Pain—1,600 died here."

This is the headquarters of Common Ground Relief, a collective of volunteers working to assist residents in rebuilding their homes, providing medical care, basic supplies, and legal assistance. By late 2007, Common Ground had assisted 170,000 people, according to Malik. It is part of a growing grassroots movement that is fighting on behalf of the thousands of residents who have been pushed out and shunned as New Orleans is redeveloped. People are demanding that their homes be restored, public schools be reopened, and public housing be unlocked.

Two hundred years ago, New Orleans was the scene of the largest slave rebellion in American history. That spirit of resistance lives on, as African-American communities are locked in a battle not just for survival, but for justice.

Abandoned . . . and Fighting

In the aftermath of Hurricane Katrina, it took days for the world to fully comprehend that the richest country on earth had abandoned and even turned on the citizens of one of its great cities. It took Malik Rahim only a few hours to size up what was happening. "This is criminal," he wrote in a message that flew around the Internet. "If you ain't got no money in America, you're on your own."

One side effect of the government's non-response was that the American media, which had been led on a short leash by the military in Iraq for the previous two years, suddenly floated free of Bush administration handlers and broadcast raw images of suffering from the darkened, flooded city. This is what unembedded journalism looks like. But racism colored both the media coverage and relief efforts.

In Rahim's neighborhood of Algiers, which was not flooded, he watched as armed white vigilantes roamed the neighborhood in pickup trucks, menacing and shooting at African-Americans. New Orleans after Katrina resembled an armed camp—and black people were the prisoners. Rahim observed bitterly right after the storm, "If a white person was taking something, he was taking food for his family. But if a black was taking something, he was looting."

In the days following the hurricane, *Democracy Now!* reported live from the devastated area. Two weeks after the storm, Malik pointed out a dead body that had been rotting on the sidewalk, ignored by the authorities who were passing by all day. "I wouldn't care if it's Saddam Hussein or bin Laden. *Nobody* deserve to be left here," he said, gently moving a piece of corrugated metal to cover the corpse. "This is what is frightening a lot of people into leaving."

"We done talked to everyone from the army to the New Orleans Police to the state troopers to—I mean, we done talked to everybody who we can," said Malik, waving his hand in front of his face in a futile effort to repel the stench of decay. "It's two weeks—*two weeks*—that this man been just layin' here."

As if on cue, every level of occupying authority appeared on the scene—but no one did anything. *Democracy Now!* asked soldiers from Fort Hood, Texas, who were standing nearby, if they could pick up the dead body.

"I don't think we can pick it up, but we can call the local authorities to come pick it up," replied the commanding officer. Just then, Louisiana State Troopers cruised by. Could they pick up the dead body?

"You need to talk to our public information officer, ma'am," replied the officer with a sarcastic smile, refusing to reveal his name. To every question and attempt to get help, he repeated the same answer, five times in all, like a broken record.

Then a New Orleans Police cruiser pulled up. Would they move the corpse? "I have no comment on that, ma'am. You have to call one of the press guys. Sorry. Thank you." And the officers drove off.

The soldiers watched all this from the roadside. One said he was from California and had returned from Iraq five months earlier. How did Iraq compare with New Orleans? Capt. Matthew Cohen replied, "It's great that we can kind of come out and actually help Americans."

Rahim fought back against official neglect in the way he knew best: He organized. Taking a page from his days as a Black Panther—when the party established drug-free zones in the housing projects, did cleanups, and fed as many as five hundred children each morning—he confronted racism and poverty by preaching a message of self-reliance and black pride, and by providing social services. "Self-sufficiency has been a policy that's guided me all of my life," he tells us. "Because you could never be a true man if you are dependent on others for your livelihood."

Faced with the stunning reality that he and many of his neighbors would have to survive on their own, Rahim published his phone number on the Internet with a plea for "calls from old friends and anyone with questions or ideas for saving lives." It was a desperate shot in the dark. But he knew that no one was coming to save them.

Meanwhile, he armed himself to defend against the white vigilantes who were on the loose. When one of the vigilantes threatened to burn down his house, Malik told him he would go down fighting. "It ain't no fun when the rabbit got a gun," he warned one of them.

Within days, two large white guys were at his door. "We're looking for Malik," said one. Figuring they might be vigilantes, Malik reached for the weapon by his door. "I figured if they gonna pull out a gun, I was gonna kill 'em," he said. What happened next stunned him.

"My name is Bear, and I'm with Veterans for Peace," declared one of the men. Rahim, himself a Vietnam vet, had been on a peace mission to Iraq with this group of anti-warriors. The old soldiers exchanged bear hugs. Then they made a plan and got to work. Within days, Veterans for Peace brought truckloads of supplies. "That was the first supplies we got. They brought us generators, boats. That helped us to survive through Katrina and [Hurricane] Rita."

One by one, more help arrived at Malik's door. Doctors came, ready to volunteer. College kids showed up, eager to distribute food and gut and rebuild homes. A movement was taking shape. But how to harness all this goodwill?

One night, the assembled activists were debating on the porch about why so many social movements fail. They concluded that they "allow our petty difference to stop us from working together," recounts Rahim. Robert King Wilkerson, a former Black Panther who had recently been released from death row in Louisiana's notorious Angola Prison, told the activists, "What you need to find is common ground that you agree to work under." Thus was born Common Ground Relief.

Common Ground began with three volunteers and $50. Within days, it opened up a medical clinic in a mosque in Algiers. After receiving a $40,000 donation from filmmaker Michael Moore, Common Ground opened a distribution center to provide food, water, and supplies to the thousands of low-income residents who were unable to evacuate. As official agencies such as FEMA and the Red Cross turned away volunteers, many veterans, peace activists, students, and ordinary citizens flocked to the grassroots aid operation of Common Ground.

For the abandoned, suffering knew no bounds. Common Ground crisscrossed class and racial divides, becoming among the first to provide relief to Latino neighborhoods and to the Native American community. "We even served the families of the vigilantes," says Rahim. "Some of the politicians had to come to us for supplies, even though we can't get no help out of them."

In addition to its distribution center and medical clinic, Common Ground now has a legal clinic, and volunteers have come from around the world to its headquarters in the Lower Ninth Ward to help gut and rehab flooded homes. In the spirit of their slogan—"solidarity, not charity"—Common Ground volunteers also train local residents to rebuild their own homes.

Rick Jay, a retired high school teacher from Minnesota, was taking a break one morning in the air-conditioned "chill room" where the forty volunteers share meals and use computers. He had been with Common Ground for six months. "I knew people were distressed here and I wanted to do all I could do to help," he tells us. A woman sitting next to him was a college freshman from Oregon, and another woman had come from France.

We ask Malik whether he sees any irony in having white volunteers be at the center of his black self-reliance scheme. "I think history will recall this as the greatest humanitarian effort by Americans to Americans. Never before in the history of this state have you had thousands of whites come down into a black community that didn't come as exploiters or oppressors," he replies. "They have brought justice."

Profiting from Disaster

"Don't believe the hype: Gulf Coast recovery is not 'slow'—it's a privatization scheme that takes away our homes, schools, hospitals and human rights."

This T-shirt slogan captures what is happening in New Orleans, which has become a national laboratory for right-wing social and economic policies. New Orleans's disaster was transformed into a windfall for Bush's cronies, as major relief and recovery efforts were handed over to politically connected private companies. The funeral company Kenyon, a division of Service Corporation International, a large donor to President Bush, was paid $12,500 per corpse that it retrieved.[4] Of the $2.3 billion in contracts awarded by the federal government in the weeks following the hurricane, more than 80 percent were awarded with little or no competition, and much of the money flowed to firms with deep connections in the Bush administration. AshBritt Environmental, which won a $568 million contract with the Army Corps of Engineers for debris removal, is a client of Barbour, Griffith and Rogers, the high-powered Washington lobbying firm and namesake of Mississippi Gov. Haley Barbour, the chairman of the Republican National Committee from 1993 to 1996. AshBritt employees contributed $30,500 to federal candidates, parties, and political action committees from 1999 to 2004, nearly 90 percent of which went to Republicans.[5]

Then there were the familiar names of Kellogg Brown and Root ($128,000 in federal electoral contributions, 1999–2004, 91 percent to Republicans), owned by Halliburton, which was run by Dick Cheney before he entered the White House. KBR received $60 million in Gulf cleanup contracts. KBR was represented by Joe Allbaugh, the ex–FEMA director who was Bush's presidential campaign manager in 2000. Allbaugh also represented Shaw Environmental ($224,824 in federal electoral contributions, 1999–2004, 46 percent to Republicans, plus $100,000 to Bush's 2005 inaugural committee),[6] which landed $200 million in cleanup contracts.

Where money flowed, scandal followed. Congressional

Democrats criticized the $575 million contract that Bechtel Corporation received to deliver and install 36,000 trailers in southern Mississippi, charging, "Despite the high cost, the delivery of trailers was much too slow and horribly inefficient."[7] The FEMA trailers have since been found to be poisoning occupants with toxic emissions of formaldehyde.

Some Hurricane Katrina contractors were just floating on money. Take Carnival Cruise Lines, which won a $236 million six-month contract for three of its ships to house hurricane evacuees. The ships sat half-empty in the Mississippi River and Mobile Bay. The government paid $1,275 per week per evacuee to stay on the ships. But if you were a vacationer, you would have paid less than half that amount: a weeklong Caribbean cruise from Texas cost $599 on Carnival. This amazing waste makes more sense when you learn that Carnival's employees and its PAC have contributed $994,800 to federal candidates, party committees, and PACs between 1999 and 2004, 58 percent of which went to Republicans.[8]

The plunder of New Orleans that followed Hurricane Katrina was especially brutal in the public sector. Rarely have those who rely on public institutions lost so much, so fast. The Bush administration refused to pay municipal workers' salaries with emergency funds, so three thousand city employees were fired. Schools have been especially hard hit: All public school teachers were summarily fired after the hurricane. The State of Louisiana took control of the New Orleans schools in November 2005, and quickly began privatizing them. More than 70 percent of New Orleans schools have reopened as charter schools run by for-profit or nonprofit organizations, many of which have selective admissions.[9] Students who can't make the grade at the charter schools can attend what is called the Recovery School District, the skeletal remains of public education in New Orleans. The number of unionized teachers has dropped from 4,700 before Katrina to 1,200 today.[10] John Mc-Donogh Senior High School in New Orleans reopened with 35 security guards, but only 23 teachers.

Poor people have taken the hardest hit in the area of housing. Hurricane Katrina drove out more than half of the residents of New Orleans. By 2007, only two-thirds of the city's pre-Katrina population had returned. The poorest have suffered the brunt of the upheaval: Of the 5,100 families who lived in public housing, less than one-quarter of them have been able to return home. That's because many of them have no homes to return to—not because their homes were irreparably damaged, but because New Orleans doesn't want its poorest residents back.

In September 2007, the Housing Authority of New Orleans (HANO) received final permission from the Bush administration to demolish its four largest public housing developments and replace them with mixed-income housing. More than 4,600 units of public housing would be lost at a time when an acute shortage of rental housing in the city has caused rents to double. The demolitions are part of a plan pushed by U.S. Housing and Urban Development Secretary Alphonso Jackson in the aftermath of Katrina. The demolitions coincide with the closure of all FEMA trailer camps around the city by May 2008, pushing nine hundred families out of their homes. This plan has delivered immediate results: By early 2008, the number of homeless people in New Orleans had doubled to about twelve thousand.[11]

Tracie Washington, an attorney and president of the

Louisiana Justice Institute, explained to us, "Some of these developments that are closed down took in no water. I mean, they were not damaged at all. Lafitte [housing project]? No water. C.J. Peete? No water. But the decision was made to take advantage of an opportunity. Hurricane Katrina came, [and] look what we can do: We can keep these people away from here, bring in the bulldozers, tear down this housing, cut the unit space and occupancy by two-thirds, call it mixed-income, take that one-third that's left and divide it into three. So we have a third of that space for public housing residents, and the rest we will use for market rate and a little bit below market rate. And that has always been the plan."

In spite of being dispersed, distressed, and disenfranchised, public housing residents are in a fight for their lives to return. It is a battle that has grown increasingly desperate.

On August 31, 2007, two dozen public housing residents and activists from around the country took over the HANO offices in New Orleans. They demanded a meeting with housing officials to discuss returning to their apartments in the public housing projects. They were met by a massive show of armed force: When we arrived, we witnessed National Guardsmen, police SWAT teams, and dozens of New Orleans Police squad cars ringing the HANO offices, which had been closed down. After several tense hours inside, the protesters emerged, singing and chanting.

Sharon Sears Jasper, a 58-year-old resident of the St. Bernard housing development, explained to reporters who had gathered outside: "Today we are here to let you know that we are not going to stop. There will be no peace until we have justice. We refuse to let you tear our homes down and continue to destroy our lives. The government, the president of the United States—you all have failed us. . . . It's two years after the storm, and we are still suffering. . . . Our people are dying of stress, depression, and broken homes. We demand that you open all public housing."

When a reporter asked her why she couldn't live somewhere else, Jasper, a large, strong-willed woman with a booming voice, shot back, "How you feel if someone tells you you can't go back to *your* home? It might not be fancy, but it's my home."

She lectured the assembled reporters, with police hovering in the background. "We are working-class people, not animals. We are a community. We work together, play together, and pray together."

The housing protest took place against a backdrop of activism around hurricane relief. In downtown New Orleans that day, activists had gathered for the International People's Tribunal on Hurricane Katrina and Rita, to hear testimony from people affected by the hurricane and its aftermath. The five-day gathering was organized by the People's Hurricane Relief Fund, a community organization working on housing, health care, and other issues, and cosponsored by Common Ground Relief, the National Conference of Black Lawyers, and other organizations. The tribunal brought together hurricane survivors, international delegations, expert witnesses, a team of human rights and civil rights attorneys, and a panel of U.S.-based and international judges. One survivor of the hurricane, Viola Washington, said, "We are calling for an international tribunal to bring charges of racial discrimination, forced eviction of public housing residents, violations of the right to life and health, and the denial of the right to return."

Tracie Washington, who has filed a lawsuit on behalf of public housing residents seeking to get back into the

St. Bernard housing project, recalled how rumors were flying that the city was planning to replace public housing with golf courses. "I'm like, 'Okay, sure . . . They want to put golf courses right in the middle of the 'hood.' And you'd hear it, and you'd basically dismiss it." Then rumor became reality. "Just this summer, the plans were announced for what the developers plan to do with St. Bernard. And guess what? Two championship golf courses in that development." She says with a bitter smile, "Now I guess we just fight to get them on the back nine."

Blacks who are displaced and homeless feel that the intent of the policy is unmistakable. "This is just part of that whole gentrification program and the changing of the demographics of the city," charges Malcolm Suber, national organizing coordinator for People's Hurricane Relief Fund, which is fighting to obtain rebuilding funds that were promised to residents from the state and the Red Cross. More than half of the applicants for federal "Road Home" money that was earmarked for people to rebuild their homes had not received any assistance as of late 2007.

Suber says, "The local white ruling class wants to regain its political control, and so they have used this storm and the flooding as a convenient excuse to get rid of black folk, especially poor black people. And basically their mentality is, 'You can only come back to this plantation if you've got a job. If you don't have a job, we don't want to provide any social services.'"

Suber's view was confirmed early on by Republican Congressman Richard Baker from Baton Rouge, who was overheard telling lobbyists just days after Katrina devastated the city: "We finally cleaned up public housing in New Orleans. We couldn't do it, but God did."[12]

Any lingering doubt about the drive to gentrify and whiten New Orleans was erased after local elections in November 2007. For the first time in twenty years, whites won a majority of seats on the City Council. White candidates also took a judgeship and two New Orleans seats in the Louisiana legislature that had long been held by blacks. Less than half the number of people voted in 2007 as voted in the New Orleans mayoral election in May 2006. Reporting on the 2007 election, the *New York Times* observed, "New Orleans became almost overnight a smaller, whiter city with a much reduced black majority."[13]

In December 2007, protesters gathered at a New Orleans City Council meeting to demand that the city intervene to halt the imminent demolition of public housing. The City Council president stopped the meeting after protesters began chanting and shouting. Police then grabbed civil rights attorney Bill Quigley, a leader of the legal fight against the demolitions, and shoved him up against the wall. He was handcuffed and charged with disturbing the peace. Quigley declared after being released, "We live in a system where if you cheer or chant in the City Council you get arrested, but you can demolish 4,500 people's apartments and everybody's supposed to go along with that? That's not going to happen. There's going to be a lot more disturbing the peace before this is all over."[14]

Five-year-old Nigel, his hair braided tightly against his scalp, tells us, "I wanna go home." Clinging to the leg of his grandmother, Stephanie Mingo, a resident of St. Bernard, he says plaintively, "I wanna go back to St. Bernard. I miss my home."

We ask him what he will do when he returns. "The first thing I'm gonna do, I'm gonna have a party."

"For real?" we ask.

"Yeah, for real, for real!" he says, breaking into a wide smile.

On December 20, 2007, the New Orleans City Council voted unanimously to move ahead with the demolition of 4,500 units of public housing. Protesters were shot with pepper spray and Tasered inside the City Council chambers.

Malik Rahim walks along an empty sidewalk in the Lower Ninth Ward and pauses at a plastic bucket where a small sapling is sitting in water. "We growin' trees to stop the erosion of our wetlands," he explains. Common Ground has already planted fifteen thousand indigenous trees as part of this effort. He strolls over to a large garden plot and notes that they are spraying bacteria and growing sunflowers and mustard grass, all of which detoxify the soils, which have high concentrations of lead and arsenic. He points with pride to the food that volunteers are growing nearby. "That shows we know what we doin' with our soil remediation."

The sweat now running off his brow and soaking his T-shirt, Malik keeps going. He is on a mission—but his sights are set far beyond the bayous of New Orleans. He shows us a large two-story house that volunteers have gutted and repaired. Inside are boxes of clothes. "We are keeping these to send to Haiti. There are those that are even less fortunate than us." There are also stacks of cots, and outside, there is a refrigerator truck.

"I want Common Ground to become a global organization," he declares as we stand in a barren lot where vegetables are now growing. "We had volunteers from twenty nations. I would like to go back and extend support to those individuals and nations who helped us. Right now, we could serve five thousand people from any disaster with meals, sanitation, communications, a health clinic, and we could help provide for children."And Common Ground did just that. When huge fires broke out around San Diego in October 2007 that forced the evacuation of a half million people, Malik and eight Common Ground volunteers were there assisting displaced Latinos, many of them undocumented workers. "We went to help those that our country refused to help," he says.

It is an audacious proposition, that people with so many needs can reach out and help others in greater need. It's a sign that in the Lower Ninth and elsewhere on the Gulf Coast, the storms can never vanquish the hope and determination of long suffering people to reclaim their common ground.

CHAPTER 2

T Is for Terrorist

Growing up in Iraq under Saddam Hussein in the 1990s, Raed Jarrar knew that people could be stopped and interrogated—and worse—on a whim. Perhaps a suspicious neighbor might report him. Maybe a cop didn't like the way he looked. So he and his family kept their heads down and stayed out of trouble.

When Jarrar became a U.S. citizen in 2006, he figured those days were behind him. America touted its freedoms, among them the freedom from arbitrary arrest and harassment. All this changed on August 12, 2006.

The olive skinned 28-year-old Iraqi-born man with a short goatee was walking to his flight in JFK Airport in New York that day. He had just cleared the security area and went to get some breakfast. Jarrar, an Iraqi architect, blogger, and peace activist, was feeling tired and looking forward to some rest and relaxation at his home in Oakland. As he sat down to enjoy his coffee, two officials suddenly accosted him. One of them quickly flashed a badge and told Jarrar to follow him.

The man asked for his boarding pass and identification. Jarrar was nervous: What had he done?

Over at the JetBlue counter, the man, who Jarrar learned was Inspector Harris from the Transportation Security Administration (TSA), was joined by a JetBlue agent. "You can't board the plane," Inspector Harris announced. Other people began to swarm.

"What's the problem?" asked a shocked Jarrar.

"It's your T-shirt," said Inspector Harris. Jarrar was wearing a black T-shirt with the inscription "We Will Not Be Silent" in both Arabic and English. The shirt had recently been given to him at a rally in Washington, D.C., by the group Artists Against the War. Harris demanded to know what the Arabic said. Jarrar explained that it said the same thing as it did in English. Harris said he couldn't be sure, because they didn't have a translator.

"Wearing a T-shirt with Arabic script in an airport now is like going to a bank with a T-shirt that reads, 'I am a robber,' " a JetBlue official informed him.

"I am ready to put on another T-shirt if you tell me what is the law that requires such a thing. I want to talk to your supervisor," demanded Jarrar.

"You don't have to talk to anyone," Inspector Harris replied. "Many people called and complained about your T-shirt. JetBlue customers were calling before you reached the checkpoint."

"Isn't it my constitutional right to express myself in this way?" Jarrar asked.

"People here in the U.S. don't understand these things about constitutional rights," a JetBlue agent replied.

"I live in the U.S., and I understand it is my right to wear this T-shirt," Jarrar protested.

Security officials then debated what kind of T-shirt to get for Jarrar. One suggested a T-shirt that said "I Love NY." But Inspector Harris intervened with his own brand of cultural sensitivity. "We don't want to take him from one extreme to another," he said.

"Why do you think that I don't love New York just because I was wearing an Arabic T-shirt?" Jarrar challenged him.

Finally, a JetBlue official bought Jarrar a T-shirt that said "New York" and insisted that he put it on.

A nervous and humiliated Jarrar reluctantly complied with demands that he change shirts. Throughout this confrontation, he had another Arab man on his mind: Maher Arar. Arar is a Syrian-born Canadian citizen who was arrested at JFK Airport in September 2002 while in transit back home to Canada. U.S. authorities secretly deported him to Syria, where he spent a year in a grave-like cell being tortured and interrogated at the behest of the Bush administration, before finally being released. No charges were ever filed against him, and a Canadian government inquiry completely exonerated him. In 2007, the Canadian government paid Arar $10 million to compensate for its role in his false arrest by the United States.

A chastened Jarrar, wearing a newly purchased T-shirt, awaited his flight. But airline officials were not done with him: JetBlue officials motioned him over and then tore up his boarding pass. Jarrar had a seat at the front of the plane. But the agent handed him a boarding pass for a seat at the back of the bus—er, plane—next to the toilets. He was ordered to board the plane alone, before passengers with disabilities or small children. It was the final humiliation for a man whose only crime was wearing a T-shirt with Arabic script.

Raed Jarrar and his family have firsthand experience of U.S. foreign policy. The son of an Iraqi mother and a Palestinian father, both engineers, Raed was born in Baghdad in 1978. His family moved between Jordan and Saudi Arabia before settling in Iraq again in 1990, where Raed attended high school and college. He and his family were in Baghdad when the United States invaded in 2003, but they were forced to flee to Jordan when fighting became too intense. His mother still returns to Iraq for work each month.

The pleasant neighborhood where Raed lived in Baghdad is now a war zone. There is no running water or electricity. Everyone in his family has had close calls in recent years. Raed was briefly detained and interrogated by a militia group; his mother was held up at gunpoint and had her car stolen; and in what he says was the final straw for the family, his brother Khalid was arrested and secretly detained by Iraqi agents from the Ministry of the Interior. For two weeks, the family thought Khalid was dead. His father visited morgues in an effort to find his body. Khalid was at last able to make a call from jail to tell his family that he was alive. When Khalid was finally brought before a judge (after the family paid thousands of dollars in bribes), they learned that he was charged with communicating with foreign terrorists. The proof? He was caught reading a blog that was critical of the Iraqi government—it was Raed's popular blog, "Raed in the Middle." The Iraqi judge released Khalid, saying there was a difference between criticism and terrorism—a distinction that is evidently lost on the U.S. government.

In spite of these close calls, Jarrar is doing better than most Iraqis. "About 4.5 million Iraqis have fled their homes in the last four years—2.2 million people outside the country, and 2.2 million inside the country," Raed reflected about his plight. "So I can't complain about this."

Raed married an Iranian-American woman and moved with her to the United States in August 2006. He decided that working for peace was more important than working as an architect, which he was trained to do. So he took a job as the Iraq project director with Global Exchange, a San Francisco–based peace and justice group. At the time he was passing through JFK Airport, he was returning from a trip to Jordan with U.S. peace activists. They had met with members of the Iraqi parliament to discuss reconciliation and alternative solutions to the American occupation. "We wanted to find other channels in dealing with the Iraqi government other than [Iraqi president] al-Maliki and the few people around him, who are repeating the same Bush administration lies and excuses for keeping the troops there," he said.

"We Will Not Be Silent"—the phrase on the black T-shirt—immediately resonated with Jarrar when he saw it at a peace rally. "I am an architect who decided to put his career on the side and just work to expose the crimes happening to Iraqis, Palestinians, or Iranians, and the abuses of human rights that are happening worldwide or in the U.S.," he told us. "This administration managed to push me out of my home and my country. But they will never manage to silence me. I will continue speaking and try to be effective in changing the U.S. policy that destroyed the lives of people around the world. That's why this is an important message: We will not be silent watching this government abusing human

rights and breaking international law. We will try to do something to change it.

"It is my responsibility to not be silent," he said. "My responsibility is to bring the voices of millions of people
around the world who are saying clearly a very simple message: Leave us alone. We want to have the right to self-
determine our future."

Jarrar was not aware that the phrase "we will not be
silent" originated with the White Rose resistance movement in Nazi Germany (see Introduction). He mused that
this "made it even more ironic to be silenced by this administration."

On the day he headed to JFK Airport, Jarrar wasn't actually intending to make a statement. In fact, he didn't even realize what T-shirt he was wearing until the TSA agent
pointed it out. "The reason I put it on that day," Jarrar told
us sheepishly, "was because it was clean."

Profiles in Racism

Racial profiling has a long and disreputable history in the
United States. During World War I, Woodrow Wilson's attorney general, A. Mitchell Palmer, launched a vast roundup
of immigrants and leftists, many of them from Eastern Europe and many of them Jews. The notorious Palmer Raids resulted in mass detentions and deportations. Numerous people
were held without charge for months.

We've come a long way—backward. In February 2001,
President Bush declared to Congress, "Racial profiling is
wrong and we will end it in America."

Just seven months later, the Bush administration made racial profiling the official policy of the U.S. government.

In the wake of the 9/11 attacks, the administration embarked on the most sweeping roundup of immigrants since the internment of 120,000 Japanese-Americans in World War II. Federal agents and local police began to stop, interrogate, detain, and deport people without criminal charge, often for long periods, merely because of their national origin, ethnicity, or religion. As the ACLU detailed in its study *Sanctioned Bias:*

> The roundup and incarceration of thousands of men were carried out under an unprecedented veil of secrecy, leaving wives, children, classmates and employers wondering where these people had been taken, and who would be next. The Federal Bureau of Prisons imposed a communications blackout that prevented the detainees from contacting family, friends, the press and even attorneys. And in another act of almost unprecedented secrecy, the attorney general ordered that the deportation hearings of immigrants deemed of "special interest" to the government be closed to the public and the press, effectively concealing all immigration hearings of Arabs and Muslims. In a scenario eerily reminiscent of the "disappearances" of labor and student activists in Argentina during the 1980s, Arab, Muslim and South Asian men were plucked off the streets of American cities. America now had its own "disappeared."[1]

Does racial profiling make us safer? Hardly: "Of the 80,000 Arabs and Muslim foreign nationals who were required to register after September 11, the 8,000 called in for FBI interviews, and the more than 5,000 locked up in preventive detention, not one stands convicted of a terrorist crime today," notes Georgetown University law professor David Cole. "In what has surely been the most aggressive national campaign of ethnic profiling since World War II, the government's record is 0 for 93,000."[2]

Racial profiling is not unique to Arab-Americans or Muslims. Many African-Americans are familiar with the most common traffic infraction they are likely to experience: DWB—"driving while black or brown." Black drivers are three times as likely—and Hispanic drivers are twice as likely—to be searched as white drivers, a 2007 Justice Department study revealed.[3] There are similar hazards when walking, flying, or just shopping. In New York City, where one-fourth of the population is African-American, blacks comprise nearly two-thirds of all persons stopped by the New York Police Department Street Crime Unit.[4]

Being Muslim or appearing to be of Middle Eastern descent has been particularly hazardous to one's health since September 11, 2001—especially for those attempting to "fly while Muslim." In the torrent of xenophobia that has followed the attacks, Arabic has been declared a de facto official terrorist language. Wear it, read it, or speak it, and the result will be the same: You will be targeted. Consider a few of the airplane incidents that occurred in 2006 around the same time that Raed Jarrar was singled out at JFK Airport:

- British passengers demanded that two men be removed from a flight in the UK when the men began speaking Arabic.

- An Arab-Canadian doctor was barred from a flight after saying Muslim prayers before boarding.
- In November 2006, a half dozen Muslim imams were ordered off a U.S. Airways flight and detained in Minneapolis after passengers complained they were speaking in Arabic and exhibiting "suspicious behavior." They had been saying their evening prayers.

Raed Jarrar received death threats after speaking out about what happened to him. A National Guard member who served in Iraq wrote to him, "You fools you know nothing about life and freedom. If I run across you in my daily tasks, I will kill you. GET THE FUCK OUT OF MY COUNTRY IF YOU DON'T LIKE IT HERE."

The author of this screed included his full name and army e-mail address. "What is more shocking and scary than his e-mail is the fact that he doesn't even feel that he should hide his threats or his name," Jarrar wrote about the incident.

So Raed e-mailed him back: "The U.S. is my country now, as much as it's yours, or maybe a little bit more. I will do my best to make this country, our country, a better place. This may include putting people like you in jail." When the guardsman realized his identity was known, he apologized to Jarrar and begged for forgiveness.

The racial profiling stories just keep rolling in. In August 2007, the FBI in Seattle released a photo of two Middle Eastern–looking men on a ferry. Or maybe they were Italian. Or Latino. Whatever—the FBI trusted people to make the connection that these men were up to no good. The men had been spotted "exhibiting unusual behavior" while riding ferries and were "overly interested in the workings and layout" of the boats. A ferry captain snapped the photo. One man appears smiling, but the other, who bears a striking resemblance to 9/11 hijacker Mohammed Atta (don't they all?), is shown looking menacingly at the camera. The FBI said the men were taking photos and looking around the boat. The feds asked local media outlets to broadcast and print the photos in the hopes that someone could identify the men. The men were not suspects in any crime.

Suspicion. About a couple of brown-skinned guys. That's all it took for TV stations and the *Seattle Times* to plaster the city with the image of the men. But the *Seattle Post-Intelligencer,* to its credit, refused to publish the photo. Managing editor David McCumber explained in the *P-I*, "We have no confirmation that these men's behavior was anything but innocuous, and to forever taint them by associating them with terrorism under these circumstances is not consistent with our policy." Months later, the men had not been identified.

P-I columnist Robert L. Jamieson, Jr., wrote, "The authorities had fear as an ally. . . . The feds enlisted the public—like Orwellian lackeys—to be the eyes and ears of agents who have wrongly singled out people before."

Brandon Mayfield learned what happens when you are falsely accused. A lawyer in Portland, Oregon, and a convert to Islam, Mayfield was mistakenly linked by the FBI in May 2004 to a fingerprint found near the Madrid terrorist bombing two months earlier that killed 191 people—despite the insistence of Spanish authorities that Mayfield's fingerprints did not match what they had. But the FBI, using the expanded surveillance powers of the USA PATRIOT Act, had all the evidence it needed to convince itself of Mayfield's guilt: phone calls that he made to Islamic charities and incriminating evidence that agents took when they broke into Mayfield's home without his knowledge. This included a Koran and "Spanish documents"—which turned out to be his son's Spanish homework.[5]

Mayfield, who has been an outspoken critic of the Bush administration and its war on terror, spent two harrowing weeks behind bars. He was shackled, chained, and placed in a five-by-eight-foot maximum security cell. He was allowed out for one hour per day.

Within hours of Mayfield's arrest, headlines blared his crime and linked him to one of Spain's worst terrorist crimes. "The suspicion leading up to the arrest, the arrest [itself, and] the time that I spent in jail in shackles and chains . . . [was] the hardest time that myself and my family have had to endure ever," he told *Democracy Now!*

Mayfield was ultimately exonerated and received a rare public apology from the FBI. He declared, "I believe I was singled out and discriminated against, I feel, as a Muslim."

Mayfield took his fight for justice further, suing the federal government for false arrest and challenging the legality of key parts of the USA PATRIOT Act that permitted secret searches and wiretapping. In 2006, a court awarded him $2 million in damages for the false arrest. And in September 2007, in a major blow to the Bush administration, an Oregon judge struck down two pillars of the PATRIOT Act that the FBI used to conduct warrantless secret searches against Mayfield.

"For over 200 years, this nation has adhered to the rule of law with unparalleled success. A shift to a nation based on extra-constitutional authority is prohibited, as well as ill-advised," wrote U.S. district judge Ann Aiken.[6]

Stalked, vilified, burglarized, terrorized, locked down, isolated, and exonerated—this is the real face of racial and religious profiling in the United States. Unlike Brandon Mayfield, many victims are not fortunate enough to be freed.

As columnist Robert Jamieson, Jr., observed, "When ignorance meets fear and simple actions become freighted with the worst of intentions, that's when it happens: Innocent people become criminals in the minds of those who see only skin-deep."[7]

Raed Jarrar was the spark that ignited a brushfire. Laurie Arbeiter of Artists Against the War, part of the activist group Critical Voice, heard Jarrar's story on *Democracy Now!* in August 2006. Her group had made Jarrar's T-shirt in March 2006 to mark the third anniversary of the Iraq invasion; it was Arbeiter who gave Jarrar his shirt. She said the idea for the T-shirts was "to respond to what was going on in this country and to what we see as an illegal war and occupation of Iraq."

Soon after Jarrar appeared on *Democracy Now!,* the T-shirt story took off. It ran on national TV, and Arbeiter's group distributed thousands of T-shirts. Artists Against the War decided to take the issue further: They would head to the airport with other members of their group "to stand in solidarity with Raed."[8]

So a group of artists wearing black T-shirts with the same "We Will Not Be Silent" slogans in English and Arabic showed up at JFK Airport with round-trip tickets to fly on JetBlue to Washington, D.C. They dispersed throughout the airport wearing their T-shirts and managed to board planes without being stopped—although many people asked them the meaning of their shirts.

Two months after Jarrar was stopped at JFK Airport,

Hunter College student Stephanie Schwartz wore a "We Will Not Be Silent" T-shirt on the Staten Island ferry in New York City. She was soon surrounded by four armed Coast Guard officials, who stared silently at her for the thirty-minute ride. As she was getting off the boat, a security guard stopped her. "Excuse me, miss, but you better not wear that shirt on the ferry again," he told her. Schwartz was taken aback and demanded an explanation.

"I don't think it's safe. This is a high-security area," he replied.

"What's unsafe about this shirt?" she asked.

"Isn't it in Arabic?" the guard asked. He added pointedly, "You remember what happened on that JetBlue flight?"

"Yeah, I remember that incident. I think it was racial profiling," Schwartz shot back.

"Well, you're not a threat to us, but someone else wearing that shirt might be," said the guard, and again warned her not to wear the shirt on the ferry. Instead, Schwartz and numerous others protested by boarding numerous ferries while wearing the T-shirts. They, too, would not be silenced.

Jarrar said he was "very shocked to see how my oppression in JFK is being used as a precedent to justify oppressing more people. It makes me feel more responsible to take this case further and try to make a precedent out of it."

In a fitting tribute to the activists who inspired them, Artists Against the War eventually printed shirts in the original German. Six decades after the words were first written as a warning about fascism, the fighting artists revived the courageous spirit of resistance of the White Rose to deliver a blow against profiling by land, by air, or by sea.

Protecting America, One T-shirt at a Time

Keeping America safe by cracking down on dissent has been a hallmark of the war on terror. As part of this effort, authorities have been ever vigilant against "T-shirt terrorists."

- Zach Guiles, 14, was suspended from Williamstown Middle/High School in Williamstown, Vermont, in May 2004 after arriving at school wearing a T-shirt that called President Bush a "Chicken-Hawk-in-Chief" who was on a "World Domination Tour"; the shirt depicted the president surrounded by pictures of cocaine and a martini glass. The school told Guiles the shirt violated its dress code. So Guiles returned the next day wearing the same shirt covered by duct tape and the word *CENSORED*. Guiles and his parents sued the school, and a federal appeals court ruled that the message of the shirt was protected under the First Amendment.

- Jeffery and Nicole Rank, a young Texas couple, were arrested on the grounds of the West Virginia state capitol on July 4, 2004, where President Bush was to deliver a speech. Their crime: They were wearing homemade T-shirts that said "Bush" inside a red circle with a slash through it—the international "banned" symbol. On the back of one of their shirts was written, "Love America, Hate Bush," while the back of the other said "Regime Change Starts At Home." When event staff and police ordered them either to leave the event or remove or cover their shirts, the Ranks replied that they had a First Amendment right to peacefully express their views. The couple was arrested for trespassing, hand-cuffed, and hauled away in a police van. The charges against them were later dismissed, and the City of Charleston, which was not a defendant in the case, apologized. The Ranks sued and were awarded $80,000 in damages.

As part of their lawsuit, the Ranks obtained a heavily redacted "Presidential Advance Manual." The manual revealed that the Bush White House had a policy of excluding dissenters from President Bush's public appearances. The manual details clever ways to keep demonstrators out of view of the press: "Designate a protest area where demonstrators can be placed, preferably not in view of the event site or motorcade route." Then there is advice on forming "rally squads" to counter the message of protesters. "These squads should be instructed always to look for demonstrators. The rally squad's task is to use their signs and banners as shields between the demonstrators and the main press platform. If the demonstrators are yelling, rally squads can begin and lead supportive chants to drown out the protestors (USA! USA! USA!)."

- Mike Ferner thought he was on safe ground. A navy corpsman during Vietnam, he had just finished participating in a protest march and was sitting and having a cup of coffee at the Jesse Brown VA Medical Center in Chicago on June 30, 2006. The VA is where vets go for help. But Ferner learned that there is no safe haven for vets who don't toe the line.

Officer Adkins, a VA cop, confronted him. "Okay, your fifteen minutes is up. You gotta go," he said. "You can't be in here protesting." The silver-haired vet was baffled. Then the officer pointed to the problem: Ferner's black T-shirt said "Veterans For Peace." It featured a picture of a dove carrying an olive branch, the logo of the national peace group.

This could mean only one thing: The aging seaman was a threat to national security.

Ferner tried to convince Adkins to go back to his duties "guarding against serious terrorists."

The officer flipped open his badge and said, "No, not with that shirt. You're protesting and you have to go." Ferner facetiously suggested the cop arrest him for his T-shirt. Within seconds, the veteran was wearing handcuffs and heading to jail. The charges: disorderly conduct, a weapons charge (Ferner was carrying a small Swiss Army knife), and criminal trespassing. He was fined $275.

"I'm sure I could go back to Officer Adkins's fiefdom with a shirt that said, 'Nuke all the hajjis,' or 'Show us your tits,' or any number of truly obscene things and no one would care.

"I have to believe that this whole country has not yet gone insane, just the government," said this veteran for peace. "This kind of behavior can't be tolerated. It must be challenged."

Shortly after the incident with Raed Jarrar, JetBlue spokesperson Jenny Dervin said that the airline took action because customers were "confused or concerned about" Jarrar's T-shirt. "In that situation, our crew members have the responsibility to create a safe environment as well as safe travel," she said. The spokesperson for JetBlue, a company that touts its consumer-friendly service, noted that Jarrar put on another T-shirt "which we purchased for him."[9] Perhaps JetBlue will make this a permanent promotion: Give up your civil liberties, and win a free T-shirt.

Raed Jarrar will not be silent. In August 2007, he and the ACLU filed a federal civil rights lawsuit against the TSA and JetBlue. The suit charges that the TSA official and JetBlue illegally discriminated against Jarrar based solely on the Arabic message on his T-shirt and his ethnicity.

"If I can give an example of how U.S. foreign policy is hitting us back home, and on the other hand how we can stand against this policy, then I will be happy," said Jarrar, now a consultant on Iraq with the American Friends Service Committee.

"I don't think what I did was extraordinary. Imagine what other activists who fought for their personal freedoms and their rights and liberties in the thirties and forties went through. Imagine people who walked to work for months to support the idea of boycotting segregated public transit, or people who were killed or tortured."

He reflected, "I just hope what I did gives an example of how the same U.S. foreign policy that destroyed my life in Iraq and made me leave my first home is oppressing my freedoms in the U.S. I hope it helps people link what the U.S. is doing out there and what is happening here. There should be a realization that 'us' and 'them' are in the same bunker."

We asked Jarrar what gives him hope. He paused for a moment to consider this, then replied, "What keeps me sane and hopeful and waking up in the morning is that the majority of people around the world don't stay silent when they know that wrong things are happening. Whether in Iraq, America, or Palestine, they try to fix it. When people start coordinating their work more, I am full of hope that things will change for the better."

CHAPTER 3

Librarians Unbound

The two visitors standing at the front door of the Library Connection, a consortium of twenty-seven Connecticut libraries that share a computer system, did not look like they had come to inquire about the latest novels. The men, one dressed in a blazer, the other in a tight T-shirt, flashed their badges and asked to speak with the boss. George Christian, the Library Connection's trim, mustachioed, and ever courteous executive director, ushered them into his office. They introduced themselves as FBI agents from the Hartford office. They proceeded to hand Christian a national security letter (NSL) demanding "any and all subscriber information, billing information and access of any person or entity" that had used computers in the twenty-seven libraries between 2 P.M. and 2:45 P.M. on February 15, 2005. The letter advised that the information was sought "to protect against international terrorism."

Christian was stunned. Libraries? Terrorism? Was this the plot of some clever new thriller? The agents assured him they meant business; they drew his attention to one line in particular. Like a children's librarian, one of them used his finger to underline the words and instructed Christian to read them carefully: The recipients of this letter could not disclose "to any person that the FBI has sought or obtained access to information or records." It was a lifetime gag order; break it, and Christian could be looking at five years in jail.

He peered through his wire-rimmed glasses at the good cop/bad cop before him, and stood his ground. "I believe this is unconstitutional," he said firmly to the agents. He told them he would fight the order. One of the agents smiled, giving him that pitying look that a bully gives the prey he is about to pulverize. The agent handed him a business card, and instructed him to have his lawyer contact the FBI.

Christian slumped into his chair. He didn't actually know how he'd fight, or whom he was fighting. And from the threatening way the NSL was worded, he didn't even know if he could call a lawyer. He decided he was obligated to inform his four-member executive committee before committing the organization to a pitched legal battle.

Christian's first call was to Peter Chase, director of the Plainville Public Library in central Connecticut. Earnest, bookish, and imbued with a strong sense of civic-mindedness, Chase is the quintessential librarian. He just couldn't say no when his fellow librarians asked him in early 2005 to serve on the board of the Library Connection. "We'll make you the vice president," a colleague said to woo him. "It'll be easy."

Two weeks later, he got a cryptic phone call from Christian. "We have a situation that requires a decision of the executive committee, and requires it right away," Christian informed him solemnly. Little did Chase realize that his volunteer work was about to morph into a nightmare with national implications.

The executive committee—Chase, Christian, Portland Public Library director Janet Nocek, and Glastonbury Public Library director Barbara Bailey—met with an attorney in the Windsor offices of the Library Connection, not far from Hartford. George Christian passed around the national security letter that the FBI agents had handed him. The attorney then announced that by virtue of having read the NSL, everyone in the room was bound by its provisions and gagged. It was as if they had been exposed to radioactivity: Once they were contaminated, they could not approach anyone.

This marked the beginning of a year-long battle that was to pit the four Connecticut librarians, barred from speaking publicly and identified only as "John Doe Connecticut," against the full might and power of the national security state. But as the Bush administration was about to learn, these librarians were not going to be so easily "shushed."

The USA PATRIOT Act, a sweeping antiterrorism law rubber-stamped by Congress three months after the 9/11 attacks, drastically eased restrictions on the issuance of national security letters, which are one of the most secretive and draconian investigative weapons used by the FBI. An NSL allows the FBI to demand phone, financial, and electronic records without court approval, and simultaneously imposes a veil of secrecy and silence over the investigation.

For the Bush administration, NSLs are the perfect weapon: no judges, no public discussion, no rights. Just a one-sided fight where the government has all the muscle.

You might think that this is an obscure tool reserved only

for hardened terrorists. Think again: A March 2007 report from the Justice Department's inspector general disclosed that more than 143,000 NSL requests were issued between 2003 and 2005. In 2000, a year before the PATRIOT Act was passed, 8,500 NSL requests were issued; by contrast, in 2004, there were 56,000 NSL requests. With unchecked power, abuse has been rampant. A June 2007 investigation revealed that the FBI had broken the law or regulations governing NSLs in more than 1,000 cases. Among the violations were: failing to get proper authorization, making improper requests under the law, shoddy recordkeeping, and unauthorized collection of telephone or e-mail records. The FBI consistently underreported to Congress the number of NSLs it issued. Of the 143,000 NSL requests, only one led to a conviction in a material support for terrorism case.[1] Even when an investigation is closed, information gained through an NSL is kept forever by the FBI.

Each month brings to light more abuses with NSLs. In October 2007, an ACLU lawsuit revealed that the Department of Defense, which has only limited authority to investigate nonmilitary personnel, misled Congress and schemed with the FBI to secretly issue hundreds of NSLs to obtain financial, telephone, and Internet records of Americans without court approval.

This has become the perfect crime: Only the victims of this abuse know how people's rights are being trampled under the guise of fighting "terrorism." Yet the victims are gagged, so no one has been able to describe their ordeal . . . until now.

When President Bush rammed the PATRIOT Act through a fearful Congress shortly after the 9/11 attacks, he could count on rolling over cowed senators and a traumatized public. But there was one adversary Bush hadn't counted on: America's librarians. These unsung guardians of democracy were about to teach a lesson to the president that they normally reserve for unruly kids in the reference section: Hell hath no fury like a librarian scorned.

Peter Chase and Janet Nocek greeted us at the door of the Plainville Public Library. Chase's smile tightened when we asked to bend the rules by bringing in our full cups of coffee. He looked around, and since the library was closed, he nodded for us to keep them with us as we headed swiftly to his tidy basement office. Despite its being after hours, he was still on duty, sporting a tie and badge that identified him as the library director.

As we walked through the library, Nocek pointed out that libraries "serve more people than McDonald's."

Chase piped in, "Libraries are one of the best loved institutions. Congress should do as well."

The beautifully renovated Plainville library would be the envy of any community. Built in 1931, the stone building with stately wooden columns serves a formerly industrial community of nineteen thousand. "We wanted people to want to walk into the building even if they couldn't read," Chase told us with the pride of a doting parent. The library is now a state-of-the-art multimedia facility with rows of public computers sharing floor space with the extensive book collection.

Public libraries have always stood for more than just books and bytes. Chase explained to us with great earnestness, "We consider ourselves to be a pillar of democracy." Central to fulfilling this role is the library's ability to assure the privacy of its patrons. "For librarians, who uses the library for what is a matter of confidence. We feel that people come to the library and they should use it for whatever they want. They should see a variety of ideas and form their own opinions." Chase added, "We feel that spying on what people are doing in libraries is like spying on people in voting booths."

But the USA PATRIOT Act (the name is an acronym for "Uniting and Strengthening America by Providing Appropriate Tools Required to Intercept and Obstruct Terrorism") is all about spying on citizens. It authorizes myriad ways for the government to eavesdrop, wiretap, and open mail and e-mail, often without court orders. The Bush administration's insatiable appetite for spying inevitably takes special aim at libraries. Section 215 of the act allows an FBI agent to enter a library or bookstore and demand records of the books that patrons read and which Internet sites they visit. The American Library Association (ALA) led the charge against this provision and has encouraged libraries to use circulation software that automatically erases any record of a patron's book use—provided the book is returned and the fines paid. So now there's added incentive to return your library books on time: If you don't, the FBI might want to talk to you.

Former attorney general John Ashcroft mocked librarians and the ALA, accusing them and other administration critics of fueling "baseless hysteria" about the government's use of the PATRIOT Act to pry into the public's reading habits. Former Justice Department spokesman Mark Carallo claimed the ALA "has been somewhat duped by those who are ideologically opposed to the PATRIOT Act," adding that Ashcroft's remarks "should be seen as a jab at those who would mislead librarians and the general public into believing the absurd, that the FBI is running around monitoring libraries instead of going after terrorists."[2]

Attorney General Michael Mukasey scoffed at the concerns of librarians, writing in 2004, "The USA PATRIOT Act has become the focus of a good deal of hysteria, some of it reflexive, much of it recreational." He chastised those "that suggest [the PATRIOT Act] gives the government the power to investigate us based on what we read, or that people who work for the government actually have the inclination to do such a thing, not to mention the spare time."[3]

Absurd to spy on libraries? The ALA knew that it was happening. A sampling of ALA members in 2005 revealed that libraries had received at least 200 requests for information from law enforcement authorities since September 11, 2001. In 147 cases, these were formal requests or came as subpoenas.[4]

Few Americans understand how draconian the PATRIOT Act is unless it reaches out and touches them. When the four Connecticut librarians received a national security letter, they were shocked to learn that it stripped away civil rights that they thought were inviolable.

"Where is the court order?" Chase asked George Christian.

"There is none," replied Christian. "They said they didn't need one because they had an NSL." The librarians were being ordered to turn over records on their patrons simply because an FBI agent told them to.

"All of us, as law-abiding citizens, understand that when there's a subpoena, and there's judicial oversight of the process in the course of an investigation, library records may be subpoenaed," said Alice Knapp, president of the Connecticut

Library Association and director of public services at the Ferguson Library in Stamford. "But what is of the utmost concern to people is the lack of oversight [in the PATRIOT Act]. And that it can be used for a fishing expedition."[5]

Chase explained, "For us, this is a very important principle. A court order protects you because you have a neutral third party—the court—and you must convince them that a crime has been committed. People come to us and say very confidential things to our reference librarians—they have medical issues, personal matters. What people are borrowing at a public library is nobody's business."

For librarians, safeguarding the privacy of their patrons is a sacred trust. Chase recounted how local police once came into the Plainville Public Library alleging that a driver in a nearby hit-and-run car accident had just come from the library. The police demanded to know who had borrowed books that afternoon so that they could identify potential suspects. "I told them to get a warrant," said Chase, whose politeness belies his steely determination. "They were not happy with me, but that's okay."

As for the cops? "They didn't get the information."

The Library Connection attorney said that the only way to avoid arrest was to either give the FBI the information it wanted, or sue the attorney general of the United States. The librarians quickly realized that they had been snared in a cynical trap. "We were well aware that Ashcroft actually said we were being 'hysterical' because [the government] was not using the PATRIOT Act against libraries," Chase told us. "So what are we supposed to do—actively participate in this deception? It was not bad enough that we had to watch this. Now we had to join in."

For Connecticut's mild-mannered librarians, there was no hesitation about how they would respond to this attack on the privacy of their patrons: They would fight like hell.

A Diabolical Deception

The four librarians decided on an aggressive legal approach. They would mount a frontal assault against the PATRIOT Act itself. They engaged the national office of the American Civil Liberties Union in New York to represent them in their lawsuit, *John Doe v. Gonzales.* They sought an injunction against having to comply with the NSL, and they wanted a broader ruling to strike down NSLs as unconstitutional. They also wanted their gag order lifted in order to be able to inform their full board of directors about what was happening. Most important, the librarians wanted to be able to participate in the national debate going on in 2005 and early 2006 over renewal of the PATRIOT Act. They thought Americans would want to know that the FBI had declared public libraries to be a front line in the war on terror.

"We were the only ones in America who could testify that they really were using [the PATRIOT Act] against libraries," said Chase. "But we couldn't speak."

The librarians learned from their attorneys that the NSL statute had already been ruled unconstitutional by a federal district court in New York in an ongoing case involving a small New York Internet service provider (ISP) that was resisting an NSL seeking information about one of its clients. The government appealed the decision, and the librarians decided to join their case with the ISP. But because of the gag order, they did not know the name or any details about the codefendant or his case.

The gag order quickly ensnared the librarians. Peter Chase was head of the intellectual freedom committee of the Connecticut Library Association. He had spoken often in that capacity about the dangers of the USA PATRIOT Act and had publicly debated the U.S. Attorney for Connecticut, Kevin O'Connor. Suddenly in July 2005, Chase fell silent on the subject. His lawyers advised him that he risked violating his gag order. "I could no longer speak about the PATRIOT Act because I'd be asked about the case against the librarians in Connecticut," he explained. "If I said, 'I can't talk about that,' it would be like waving a red flag saying, 'It's me! It's me!'"

By contrast, U.S. Attorney O'Connor was speaking so often and ardently in favor of the law that he boasted at one forum, "The PATRIOT Act is my mistress."[6] So while O'Connor traveled the state reassuring people that the PATRIOT Act was not targeting libraries and would only be used against terrorists, he was silencing one of his most articulate and effective critics—by using the PATRIOT Act against libraries. It was a diabolical deception worthy of Kafka.

Connecticut's newspapers were abuzz with news that librarians were in the dock. But no one initially knew who John Doe was, and the four librarians scrupulously avoided exposure. The first hearing of the Library Connection case took place in federal court in Bridgeport in September 2005. Notably missing from the courtroom were the plaintiffs. They had been declared a "threat to national security" and were barred from attending.

So America's most dangerous librarians observed the

proceedings by closed-circuit television inside a locked storage room in a Hartford courthouse. As they peered at the images, Chase noticed a familiar figure making the government's case: It was Kevin O'Connor. "So the very man who is having me gagged, who I debated, is making the case against me," he observed wryly.

There was something else they saw in those images from the Bridgeport courtroom: There were librarians in every row. They came from around the region to show their support. John Doe was bound and gagged, but he was not alone.

The four librarians went to great pains to shield their identities, but their cover was finally blown—due to the government's bungling. Following a judge's ruling, the government was forced to release some documents in the case, and it failed to redact all the occurrences of the name of the Library Connection and of Peter Chase. Chase promptly received a phone call from a *New York Times* reporter, with whom he spoke briefly before hanging up on her. That's when things got serious.

"I called our attorney and told him what happened. There was dead silence on the other end of the line. He said, 'I'll call you back.'" Chase recounted that the lawyer called back and explained grimly, "Well, Peter, you have to understand your situation. . . . It would be easy to find out that there was a phone call between your house and the *New York Times*. If that story comes out in the *Times*, people could get the wrong idea that you are talking." The *Times* did finally publish the name of the Library Connection on September 23, 2005. The ACLU lawyer informed Chase that they had decided to hire criminal attorneys for him—just in case. And, the lawyer added pointedly, "We think it would be best for you to leave your home so that papers can't be served on you."

So Chase assumed the life of a fugitive, on the run from his own government for the crime of defending privacy and free speech in his library. "From thereon in," said Chase, "I realized how serious this was."

Bound and Gagged

Being gagged and the target of an FBI terrorism investigation became an increasingly surreal experience.

Janet Nocek couldn't tell her husband that she was the plaintiff in a major lawsuit against the attorney general of the United States. "He read in the paper that Library Connection was fighting this, and he said, 'Oh, that's good,'" she recounted. "I told him I was going to business meetings in New York City, and he didn't ask why."

George Christian testified before the U.S. Senate in 2007 that as the executive director of a nonprofit organization, "I felt terrible I could not let anyone know that the struggle was not depleting our capital reserves and putting the corporation at risk. I could not even tell our auditors that the corporation was engaged in a major lawsuit—a direct violation of my fiduciary responsibilities. I pride myself on my integrity and openness. I worried if, knowing I was participating in this court case behind their backs, the members of the board and other library directors were starting to wonder what else I might be concealing."[7]

Peter Chase was finally confronted by his family. One day his teenage son bounded out of the house to greet him, looking ashen. "Dad, you just got a call from the Associated Press saying the FBI is investigating you. Is that *true*? Why haven't you told us?"

Chase was unsure how to respond. He didn't want to lie, but he also didn't want to confirm anything. "I'm involved in a case," he said slowly and deliberately. "I can't talk about it. And it would be best if you didn't tell anybody about that phone call."

Chase's main concern was protecting his family from learning about the NSL, lest they instantly be bound and gagged by it. "To tell your own son—he must think I was involved in drug running!" Chase shook his head, his voice trailing off as he recounted the story. "He just wondered, why was the FBI investigating his father? The less he knew, the better it was."

Even going to court involved cloak-and-dagger tactics. When "John Doe Connecticut" went to an appeals court hearing in Manhattan in October 2005, the four librarians had to conceal their reasons for attending. Their ACLU attorneys instructed the four not to enter the room together. Furthermore, they were not allowed to sit next to one another, look at one another, or look at their attorneys. Chase dressed in lawyerly black and did his best to look "dour and grim" so as not to draw any attention. John Doe New York—the Internet service provider who was a codefendant in the case—was also in the room, but they did not know who he was.

Once again, librarians from all around Connecticut turned out in force in the courtroom. "It's nice to know that other people are on your side, especially when they can't tell you that," reflected Chase. In Washington, D.C., librarians protested in support of their unnamed Connecticut colleagues by wearing gags emblazoned "NSL." Speakers at the rally included Sen. Russell Feingold (D-Wisc.), the only senator to vote against the PATRIOT Act in 2001, Rep. Jerrold Nadler (D-N.Y.), and Rep. Bernie Sanders (I-Vt.).

The government's insistence on keeping the librarians gagged became an exercise in Orwellian absurdity. The Library Connection's name was published six times in the *New York Times* alone between September and November 2005, and Peter Chase and George Christian were identified by name in numerous newspapers. Their names were also visible on court Web sites.

Meanwhile, the government was suffering legal setbacks: Judge Janet Hall ruled in September 2005 in U.S. district court in Bridgeport that the gag order violated the librarians' first amendment rights and that there was no compelling reason why revealing their names would hinder the government's investigation. The court held that the gag was preventing "the very people who might have information regarding investigative abuses . . . from sharing that information with the public"—which, it had become abundantly clear, was the main purpose of the gag order.

The Justice Department appealed Hall's decision, insisting that revealing the librarians' identities would jeopardize national security. U.S. Attorney Kevin O'Connor insisted that abandoning the gag order would undermine the government's ability to pursue terrorists. "You can't just think about this particular case," he said.[8] The ACLU and the librarians appealed to the U.S. Supreme Court for an emergency stay in order to allow the librarians to testify before Congress, which was debating reauthorization of the PATRIOT Act at that very moment. But Justice Ruth Bader Ginsburg declined to intervene.

So Congress reconsidered the PATRIOT Act without the benefit of hearing from any victims of the law's excesses. The "debate" was utterly one-sided: While the librarians were forced into silence, the Bush administration and its allies reassured Congress and the public that what was actually happening was not happening at all.

Rep. James Sensenbrenner, Jr. (R-Wisc.), then chair of the House Judiciary Committee, declared flatly in a *USA Today* op-ed piece: "Zero. That's the number of substantiated USA PATRIOT Act civil liberties violations."

Peter Chase chafed at having to sit on the sidelines while the debate raged around him. "It was well known that librarians in Connecticut were under a gag order, and a judge had ruled that my rights had been violated." Sensenbrenner's piece was "very frustrating and made me mad that I couldn't contradict what he was saying."

Janet Nocek added, "We couldn't show our face, a human face, that citizens could look at. Their rights are being violated, too, because they couldn't get that information."

George Christian watched the national debate over the PATRIOT Act with quiet fury. He thought about the two things he'd like to ask lawmakers, if only he could speak. "I wanted to ask the Congress if any of them could explain to me in their own words what they thought the difference was between a police force authorized to act in secret with no oversight, and a secret police. I couldn't see the difference.

"The second question I wanted to ask was what good they think they are doing by giving the FBI an unconstitutional tool? If the FBI actually was able to capture some nefarious people, chances are they would be let go because of the unconstitutional methods used to capture them."

For Christian, a soft-spoken man used to working behind a desk, not at a podium, the road to standing up to injustice began during the Vietnam War. Sitting in shorts and sandals on a hot summer afternoon at his house in southern Connecticut, he talked about how he became a conscientious objector to the war forty years ago. He described a leaflet that he passed out to others who were getting their pre-induction physicals in New Haven. The leaflet urged draftees to "think about what you are doing. Your country is asking you to commit murder as the price of continued membership. Realize that resistance to the draft is possible."

Christian went on to have a family and become a software designer for large companies. "I never felt I had to take a conscientious stand like that since that time," he said. "I would have led a really unremarkable life had this issue [of the PATRIOT Act] not come knocking on my door. But when the issue does come knocking at your door, you have an obligation to take a stand if you think it is wrong."

The PATRIOT Act was reauthorized in March 2006. Librarians won a few modifications in the revised bill, including a flimsy requirement that the FBI had to show "reasonable grounds" for demanding library information, a pathetically low threshold. The deeply flawed law passed the Senate by a vote of 89–10, and passed the House 280–138.

Following the reauthorization vote, part of John Doe Connecticut's case—the challenge to the NSL provision of the PATRIOT Act—was ruled to be moot, since the law had changed, albeit slightly. But the librarians and the ACLU continued to challenge their gag order, which remained in force.

Six weeks after the PATRIOT Act was reauthorized, the

Justice Department had a sudden change of heart. The librarians were not a threat to national security after all. The government informed the ACLU that they would no longer contest the librarians' demand to lift their gag order. John Doe could have his name back. His voice, too.

"That's how the four of us became the only Americans who can speak about our personal experience" as targets of a national security letter, said Chase.

Dropping the troubled case was a cynical move for the government. By lifting the gag order, the government rendered the librarians' challenge to the constitutionality of gag orders moot. "They kept us silent just so they could pass the PATRIOT Act," said Chase. "They only allowed us to speak because it would make our case go away."

Nocek, a bespectacled woman with a serious demeanor, is not prone to being overly dramatic. But she drops her restraint when talking about the Bush administration's motives in this case. "Ungagging us was like calling the fire department after the building had burned down." The librarians speculate that the Bush administration did not want their case to go to the U.S. Supreme Court, where the government had good reason to fear that it would lose.

Even when the government dropped its fight against the librarians, it insisted that the documents relating to the case remain sealed. It took an order from the U.S. Supreme Court in August 2006 to force the Bush administration to release the documents.

The full folly of this "national security" case became apparent when the "secret documents" were unsealed. Among the evidence that the government had censored: quotes from previous Supreme Court cases; clichés such as, "Once the cat is out of the bag, the ball game is over" and "the genie is out of the bottle"; copies of *New York Times* articles; and the text of the Connecticut law that guarantees the confidentiality of library records.

The government also redacted arguments made by the ACLU attorneys, as if the ideas posed a threat to national security. Among the censored legal claims was this: "Now that John Doe's identity has been widely disseminated, the government's sole basis for the gag has wholly evaporated, and there is no conceivable further justification for employing the government's coercive powers to silence American citizens during a national political debate of historic consequence."

The lead attorney for the librarians, ACLU associate legal director Ann Beeson, declared, "The documents unsealed today show the absurdity of the government's insistence that the Library Connection staff could not speak out even after the government's negligence revealed that they were the John Doe plaintiffs. The government's shameful cries of 'national security' to hide its actions from the public is an abuse of power that only makes America less safe and less free."

The librarians insist that the members of Congress who voted to reauthorize the PATRIOT Act were deliberately duped by the Bush administration. "When Congress considers laws, they should know all the facts about them," said Nocek. "But they didn't."

Unbound and Unbowed

Connecticut's librarians are now eager to be the poster children for the excesses of the PATRIOT Act. They have been tireless in their advocacy. "Because we are the only ones who can talk about it, we haven't turned down any invitations," Chase told us. "People should know what's going on." The four plaintiffs have crisscrossed the country, including Alaska, to speak about their experience.

"The idea of a gag order in a democracy is frightening," said Chase. "When people can't talk about public affairs going on because they are under a gag order, how are we supposed to have a democracy? If it happened to some small town librarians in Connecticut, it could happen to you, too."

When we asked the librarians which book on their shelves best captured their experience, they immediately mentioned *1984*. "It smacks of a *1984* kind of government. Big Brother is always watching you," said Chase referring to George Orwell's classic tale about life under a paranoid, all-controlling authoritarian regime. "They told me you don't have to be suspected of any criminal activity to be a target of an NSL. Now they can serve it on anyone. There's no court authorization needed, and they are not telling Congress what's going on. They've made themselves judge, jury, and executioner.

"I don't think this makes us safer," Chase continued. "It makes us more fearful. It makes America a more dangerous place if we can't talk about how our government works."

Janet Nocek noted a key lesson, "One thing people should realize from our case is that you can challenge it."

The groundswell that the fighting librarians started continues to build. In September 2007, a federal court in New York ruled that the entire national security letter provision of the PATRIOT Act was unconstitutional. The decision was a major blow against the Bush administration's attempts to invoke sweeping unconstitutional powers. The ruling came in response to the case of John Doe New York, the Internet service provider whose case had been joined with the librarians. Even though the FBI had dropped its demand for information from the Internet provider, it insisted on keeping him gagged. U.S. district judge Victor Marrero in New York said the secrecy requirements of NSLs are "the legislative equivalent of breaking and entering, with an ominous free pass to the hijacking of constitutional values."

Marrero cited the cautionary examples of how courts failed to act against racial segregation and the internment of Japanese-Americans during World War II. "Viewed from the standpoint of the many citizens who lost essential human rights as a result of such expansive exercises of governmental power unchecked by judicial rulings appropriate to the occasion," Marrero wrote, "the only thing left of the judiciary's function for those Americans in that experience was a symbolic act: to sing a requiem and lower the flag on the Bill of Rights."[9]

George Christian reflected on the improbable path that moved him and his three colleagues to take on the U.S. government, and win. "People think our gifted founding fathers set up this system with a bill of rights and that we are all protected. But it's human nature that people in power feel they need more power to get the job done right. . . . If you don't stand up to these encroachments on our liberties, we'll lose them.

"Each generation has to stand up for its own rights," he mused. "If we are all passive, we end up with no rights at all."

II. *Science Under* SIEGE

Standing Up to the Madness in 1971:
The Pentagon Papers

On June 13, 1971, the New York Times *began publishing a startling series of reports. The stories exposed how the U.S. government had secretly expanded its war in Southeast Asia in the 1960s and lied to the American people to cover it up. The government could not dispute the account for a simple reason: The* Times *was publishing a top secret official government report, dubbed the Pentagon Papers. It took a courageous Pentagon insider to leak the report and blow open the real story of official deceit that had led the United States into a catastrophic war. More than 58,000 Americans lost their lives in Vietnam, and more than 3 million Vietnamese died.*

Daniel Ellsberg was a military analyst working for the Rand Corporation in the 1960s when he was asked to join an internal Pentagon group tasked with creating a comprehensive, secret history of U.S. involvement in Vietnam from World War II to 1968. Ellsberg, a former Pentagon official and marine and once a strong supporter of the war, was horrified as he delved into the official deception and catalogued the untold human cost of the war. He photocopied thousands of documents and leaked them to New York Times *reporter Neil Sheehan.*

Ellsberg recounted on Democracy Now!*, "There were seven*

thousand pages of top secret documents that demonstrated unconstitutional behavior by a succession of presidents, the violation of their oath and the violation of the oath of every one of their subordinates."

President Nixon was incensed by the leak. "People have gotta be put to the torch for this sort of thing," he told his national security advisor, Henry Kissinger. "Let's get the son of a bitch in jail." Nixon's attorney general, John Mitchell, immediately got a restraining order, stopping the Times from printing the report for fifteen days. It was the first time that presses were stopped by federal court order. Ellsberg also leaked the Pentagon Papers to the Washington Post, which began running excerpts on June 18; they, too, were stopped by Mitchell. In the most famous press freedom case in American history, New York Times Co. v. United States, the Times and Post fought the injunction and won in the U.S. Supreme Court.

Daniel Ellsberg did all he could to ensure the widest possible audience for the Pentagon Papers. He leaked the report to Washington Post editor Ben Bagdikian on the condition that Bagdikian pass on a complete set of the documents to the freshman senator from Alaska, Mike Gravel, who promised to read them into the public record. Gravel personally hauled boxes containing the seven-thousand-page report into the Senate, since he worried that only he could claim senatorial immunity should he be caught with the leaked documents. His staff aides were posted as lookouts, and disabled Vietnam veterans guarded his Senate office. Gravel broke down crying in the Senate while reading the details of Vietnamese civilian deaths. But since he had begun the reading, he was legally able to enter all seven thousand pages of the once top secret Pentagon Papers into the public record. Despite intense FBI pressure, the papers were later published by Beacon Press, the publishing arm of the Unitarian Church. Together with Ellsberg, this small independent press and the antiwar senator bravely helped turn the tide of public opinion against the Vietnam War.

Ellsberg, whom Henry Kissinger once described as "the world's most dangerous man," was relentlessly pursued and harassed by the Nixon administration. Nixon ordered a break-in into the office of Ellsberg's psychiatrist in an effort to dig up information that would discredit him. The break-in became part of the Watergate scandal that led to Nixon's eventual resignation in 1974. Beacon Press was also investigated and harassed by the FBI.

Daniel Ellsberg has spent a lifetime encouraging others to take stands of conscience. "The equivalent of the Pentagon Papers exist in safes all over Washington, not only in the Pentagon, but in the CIA, the State Department, and elsewhere," he told thousands of Unitarians at a 2007 gathering to commemorate the thirty-fifth anniversary of Beacon Press's publication of the Pentagon Papers. He has advice for those who are in a position to reveal the truth. "Don't do what I did—don't wait till the war has started," Ellsberg said. "Don't wait till the bombs have fallen against Iran or, earlier, Iraq. Don't wait till the engine of this war is unstoppable. Before the war, take the risk. Reveal what you know to be the truth. Reveal the truth under the lies of your own bosses and your superiors. Obey your oath . . . not to the commander-in-chief, not to superior officers, but to the Constitution of the United States."

CHAPTER 4

Some Don't Like It Hot

As the 2004 presidential election approached, something strange began happening at the National Aeronautics and Space Administration (NASA). The normally steady flow of news releases about glaciers, climate change, pollution, and other earth sciences slowed to a trickle. An October 2004 news conference to present new information about ozone and air pollution from a new NASA satellite was ordered postponed until after the election by Glenn Mahone, then the assistant administrator for public affairs. White House appointees instructed NASA's public affairs officers to shift the focus from earth science to President Bush's stated desire to return a man to the moon, and eventually to Mars.

Political appointees at NASA had figured out a novel way to resolve the discrepancy between Bush administration rhetoric and scientific reality: They would just erase our planet.

"All of a sudden earth science disappeared," said William Patzert, a NASA scientist. "Earth kind of got relegated to just being one of the nine or ten planets. It was ludicrous."[1]

NASA's historic mission since its establishment in 1958

has been "the expansion of human knowledge of the earth and of phenomena in the atmosphere and space." Which is why global warming falls squarely within the agency's purview. From 2002 to 2006, NASA's mission statement read, "To understand and protect our home planet; to explore the universe and search for life; to inspire the next generation of explorers . . . as only NASA can."

In early February 2006, unbeknownst to most of the agency's nineteen thousand employees, the mission statement was quietly changed: The phrase "to understand and protect our home planet" disappeared. Instead, the mission became "to pioneer the future in space exploration, scientific discovery and aeronautics research."[2]

Star Trek was in. Planet Earth was toast.

Earth had to be erased for a reason: The science about Earth—namely, the alarming and incontrovertible evidence of global warming—conflicted with the fantasy being spun by President Bush and his oil industry backers that climate change wasn't really happening.

"My administration's climate change policy will be science-based," declared President Bush in July 2001. He must have meant science fiction, because from the moment the Bush administration took power in 2001, officials set out to undermine, distort, and suppress science that didn't serve their political ideology and financial backers. Vice President Dick Cheney made it clear who was setting the environmental agenda when he huddled behind closed doors with his former colleagues in the oil industry in early 2001 and virtually allowed them to write a new national energy policy to their liking. The result: the 2005 Energy Bill, which gave $16 billion in subsidies to the oil, gas, and coal industries, recommended opening the Arctic National Wildlife Refuge to oil and natural gas drilling, deregulated the electricity market, subsidized building new nuclear power plants, and dumbed down fuel economy standards for SUVs and light trucks. State Department documents from 2001 to 2004 reveal that the Bush administration thanked Exxon executives for their "active involvement" in determining climate change policy. Exxon officials, who called for more study and less regulation, insisted that the costs of joining the Kyoto Protocol "would be unjustifiably drastic and premature"—the same line taken by the Bush administration.[3] The message from the White House was clear: It was politics and money above all else. If science conflicted with politics or threatened corporate profits, the science must change.

The Bush administration has long been fighting efforts to cap greenhouse gas emissions. Bush has shrugged off major climate change initiatives, such as his announcement that the United States would not abide by the Kyoto Protocol, the international climate treaty signed by President Bill Clinton that requires developed countries to reduce greenhouse gas emissions. The United States is now the only industrialized country that has not ratified the treaty. In place of mandatory global emissions reductions, the Bush administration advocated voluntary restrictions. Bush abandoned a campaign pledge to limit carbon dioxide from power plants. And in December 2007, the United States defeated efforts to set firm targets for greenhouse gas reduction at a UN summit on global warming held in Bali, Indonesia. The United States is now the world's largest contributor to—and obstacle to reducing—global warming.

This inaction comes at a time when global warming has reached a tipping point. "What we do in the next two to three years will determine our future," said scientist Rajendra Pachauri in November 2007. Pachauri is chairman of the Intergovernmental Panel on Climate Change (IPCC), the organization of more than two thousand top international scientists associated with the United Nations that has issued the authoritative reports on global warming since 1990. The group was awarded the 2007 Nobel Peace Prize, together with former vice president Al Gore. The IPCC warned in its fourth major report in November 2007 that the world will have to stop the growth of carbon emissions within seven years and phase out carbon-emitting technologies in about four decades to avoid killing as many as a quarter of the planet's species.

The fallout from global warming is already evident. As Al Gore noted in his acceptance speech for the Nobel Peace Prize in December 2007, "In the last few months, it has been harder and harder to misinterpret the signs that our world is spinning out of kilter. Major cities in North and South America, Asia, and Australia are nearly out of water due to massive droughts and melting glaciers. Desperate farmers are losing their livelihoods. Peoples in the frozen Arctic and on low-lying Pacific islands are planning evacuations of places they have long called home. Unprecedented wildfires have forced a half million people from their homes in one country and caused a national emergency that almost brought down the government in another. . . . We, the human species, are confronting a planetary emergency."

As with all inconvenient truths, the Bush White House

has attacked the messenger, zealously attempting to silence federal climate scientists. A survey of sixteen hundred government scientists released in 2007 by the Union of Concerned Scientists and the Government Accountability Project revealed that nearly half of the scientists perceived or personally experienced the following types of political interference:

- Pressure to eliminate the words "climate change," "global warming," or other similar terms from their communications (46 percent)
- Edits during review of their work that changed the meaning of their scientific findings (43 percent)
- New or unusual administrative requirements that impair climate-related work (46 percent)
- Statements by officials at their agencies that misrepresented scientists' findings (37 percent)
- The disappearance or unusual delay of Web sites, reports, or other science-based materials relating to climate (38 percent)
- Situations in which scientists have actively objected to, resigned from, or removed themselves from a project because of pressure to change scientific findings (25 percent)[4]

The Dissenter

James E. Hansen experienced this political interference firsthand. America's preeminent scientific expert on climate change and the so-called father of global warming science, he is the longtime director of NASA's Goddard Institute for Space Studies. Hansen has been sounding the alarm about global warming for more than two decades. As a result, he has tangled with climate change deniers such as Oklahoma Sen. James Inhofe, who has called global warming a "hoax" and dismisses Hansen as a "NASA scientist and alarmist."[5] Hansen's adamance about the threat of global warming has made him a punching bag for the deniers and a target of smears. In a series of apoplectic editorials in 2007, *Investor's Business Daily* labeled Hansen "a global warming fear monger" and charged that he was engaging in partisan politics because he "had received a $250,000 grant from the foundation headed by Teresa Heinz Kerry," the wife of Sen. John Kerry, the 2004 Democratic presidential nominee.[6] This is a bizarrely conspiratorial twist on the fact that Hansen received a 2001 Heinz Award, named for Teresa Heinz Kerry's late husband, John Heinz III, the Republican senator from Pennsylvania who died in a plane crash in 1991. The award honors "the joyous American belief that individuals have both the power and the responsibility to change the world for the better." Other Heinz Award recipients include former surgeon general C. Everett Koop, soprano Beverly Sills, Apple computer founder Steve Wozniak, and children's advocate Marian Wright Edelman.[7]

Hansen's troubles deepened on December 15, 2005, when he released data showing that 2005 had been the warmest year in at least a century. Hansen called for rapid reductions in emissions of greenhouse gases. This caught the attention of the Bush administration.

The problem was not global warming. The problem was Jim Hansen.

Hansen quickly received word that his upcoming lectures,

postings on the Goddard Web site, scientific papers, and any interview requests from journalists would need to be reviewed by the NASA public affairs staff. And there was a threat: Top NASA officials relayed a warning to Dr. Hansen about "dire consequences" if he continued to make such statements. To help rein in Hansen, he was assigned his own personal political minder: a new 24-year-old presidential appointee in the NASA public affairs office named George Deutsch.

Deutsch's primary qualification for the job of muzzling the nation's premier climate scientist was that he worked as an intern in the "war room" of the 2004 Bush-Cheney reelection campaign. Once ensconced at NASA, Deutsch set about promoting what he felt was the real scientific priority of our time: ensuring that "intelligent design"—a repackaged version of creationism that posits that the universe and all forms of life are created by an "intelligent designer" (a.k.a. God)—was given prominent play in the agency's public pronouncements.

Deutsch had admonished a NASA contractor who was working on a Web presentation about Einstein for middle school students to always note that the Big Bang was merely a "theory." "The Big Bang," Deutsch e-mailed the contractor in October 2005, is "not proven fact; it is opinion." He added, "It is not NASA's place, nor should it be, to make a declaration such as this about the existence of the universe that discounts intelligent design by a creator."[8]

Dr. Hansen said flatly that he would ignore the restrictions being placed on him. "They feel their job is to be this censor of information going out to the public," he told reporter Andrew Revkin, who chronicled Hansen's battles in the *New York Times*.

NASA denied it was muzzling Hansen. "This is not

about any individual or any issue like global warming," said Dean Acosta, NASA's deputy assistant administrator for public affairs. "It's about coordination."[9]

But Hansen had been speaking out on global warming since the 1980s without restrictions. And the few scientists whose views were in line with the Bush administration seemed to operate without constraints. Hansen knew why he was being put on a short leash: Because the ultimate threat to the Bush administration is to bypass its vaunted spin machine. "Communicating with the public seems to be essential," said Hansen, "because public concern is probably the only thing capable of overcoming the special interests that have obfuscated the topic."[10]

These "special interests" were no longer government outsiders and industry hacks trying to influence policy. These hacks were now running the White House. The wall between private and public interest had simply vanished.

Take the case of Philip Cooney. For fifteen years, he was a lobbyist for the American Petroleum Institute, the trade association for the oil industry, and an aggressive opponent of limiting carbon emissions. Cooney, a lawyer, was a "climate team leader" at API—a euphemism for being a ringleader of the global warming denial movement. This is why the Bush administration felt he was perfectly qualified to oversee federal research and policy on climate change. From 2001 to 2005, Cooney served as chief of staff of the White House Council on Environmental Quality. One of his key tasks was to review and edit major government scientific reports about climate change.

Conflict of interest? Not to the Bush White House, where it was business as usual. Cooney was among friends in the

White House. George W. Bush is a failed oilman. Dick Cheney is the former CEO of Halliburton, the world's largest oil services company. Andrew Card, Bush's former chief of staff, had previously been chief lobbyist for General Motors, where he spearheaded efforts to derail stricter fuel efficiency standards for cars. Secretary of State Condoleezza Rice served on the board of Chevron for a decade. She has the distinction of being the only cabinet member to have had an oil tanker named after her.

Cooney did exactly the job he was hired to do. Rep. Henry Waxman (D-Calif.), chair of the House Committee on Oversight and Government Reform, summarized his contribution: "Mr. Cooney and his staff made hundreds of separate edits to the government's strategic plan for climate change research. These changes injected doubt in place of certainty, minimized the dangers of climate change, and diminished the human role in causing the planet to warm."

Cooney claimed that he based his editing on the "most authoritative and current views of the state of scientific knowledge." He must have overlooked the authoritative reports by the Intergovernmental Panel on Climate Change, which warned in 2001 that the 1990s had been the warmest decade in recorded history, and that global warming would "increase threats to human health" all around the world.[11]

In 2005, following revelations in the media about his past and present work, Cooney left the White House to return to a familiar haunt, taking a job as a corporate issues manager with ExxonMobil. The oil giant, whose $40 billion in profits in 2006—a sum bigger than the budgets of 123 countries— was the largest profit ever reaped by a private corporation in world history, is a leader in the global warming denial movement. From 1998 to 2006, Exxon spent $23 million funding "think tanks" and pseudo-scientific front groups that deny global warming science and block government action.[12] Exxon-Mobil also used these front groups to silence its critics: In 2003, a little known group called Public Interest Watch, which receives 95 percent of its funding from ExxonMobil, challenged the tax-exempt status of Greenpeace, which has labeled Exxon-Mobil the "No. 1 Climate Criminal" over its environmental practices. As a result, the IRS audited Greenpeace—an expensive and worrisome disruption for any organization—but found no irregularities.

John Passacantando, executive director of Greenpeace USA, told *Democracy Now!* that the climate change denial front groups "are Exxon tools. They are funded by Exxon to do Exxon's bidding, which is to continue to confuse the public in their knowledge of the enormity of what's coming on us on global warming."

ExxonMobil and Phil Cooney had long been fellow travelers, using any means necessary to deceive the public. With his latest job, Cooney had finally come back to his master.

Showdown

On March 19, 2007, Rep. Henry Waxman held a congressional hearing about political interference in climate change science. The star witnesses were Hansen, Cooney, and George Deutsch. In February 2006, Deutsch resigned his job as a NASA public affairs officer after the *New York Times* revealed that he had inflated his résumé, falsely claiming to have graduated from Texas A&M University in 2003.[13] In fact, he took courses at the school but had not graduated.

The hearing was a moment of redemption for thousands of government scientists. They watched as one of their own courageously exposed the inner workings of the Bush spin machine and defended the right of scientists to free inquiry. And the American people finally got to hear firsthand who controls the levers of power in Washington.

Here are excerpts from the hearing before the House Committee on Oversight and Government Reform:

REP. HENRY WAXMAN, Chair: There is a saying in Washington that personnel is policy. The White House appointed an oil industry lobbyist, not a scientist or climate change expert, as chief of staff at the Council on Environmental Quality. . . . The documents we have received indicate he was able to exert tremendous influence on the direction of federal climate change policy and science.

. . . It would be a serious abuse if senior White House officials deliberately tried to defuse calls for action by ensuring that the public heard a distorted message about the risks of climate change.

In addressing climate change, science should drive policy. The public and Congress need access to the best possible science to inform the policy debate about how to protect the planet from irreversible changes. If the administration turned this principle upside down with raw political pressure, it put our country on a dangerous course.

DR. JAMES HANSEN: In my written statement, I describe a growth of political interference with climate change science. . . . [That] coincides with a growth in power of the executive branch.

It seems to me that this growth of power violates principles on which our democracy is based, especially separation of powers and checks and balances.

I have no legal expertise, but I would like to raise three questions.

Number one: When I testify to you as a government scientist, why does my testimony have to be reviewed, edited and changed by a bureaucrat in the White House before I can deliver it? Where does this requirement come from? Is not the public, who have paid for the research—are not they being cheated by this political control of scientific testimony?

Second question: Why are public affairs offices staffed by political appointees? Their job, nominally, should be to help scientists present results in a language that the public can understand. They should not be forcing scientists to parrot propaganda.

Indeed, during the current administration, NASA scientific press releases have been sent to the White House for editing, as I discuss in my written testimony. If public affairs officers are left under the control of political appointees, it seems to me that inherently they become officers of propaganda.

Point number three: The primary way that the executive branch has interfered with climate science is the control of the purse strings. This is very, very effective. Last February, a year ago [just days after Hansen charged publicly that he was being muzzled by NASA], the executive branch slashed the Earth science research and analysis budget. That's the budget that funds NASA Earth science labs such as mine. They slashed it retroactively through the beginning of the fiscal year by about 20 percent. That is a going-out-of-business level of funding.

The budget is an extremely powerful way to interfere with science and bring scientists into line with political positions.

Some people have joked that at about the same time, the White House brought in a science fiction writer for advice on global warming [a reference to Bush inviting sci-fi author and global warming denier Michael Crichton to the White House in 2005]. But this is not a joking matter. We need more scientific data, not less.

Former NASA public affairs officer George Deutsch then testified about his conflict with Hansen:

GEORGE DEUTSCH: I accepted an entry level public affairs position at NASA at the age of 23 and after several months I became a public affairs officer in NASA's Science Mission Directorate, SMD.

. . . Not long after joining SMD, I became aware of Dr. James Hansen, a distinguished and internationally renowned climate scientist. I learned that Dr. Hansen disagreed with what I understood to be NASA's standard practices for responding to media requests.

Among those practices were that public affairs officers should listen to interviews as they're being conducted, that superiors can do interviews in someone's stead, and that NASA employees should report interview requests to the public affairs office.

. . . The purpose of these guidelines was to encourage agency coordination and accurate reporting.

. . . I never censored Dr. Hansen, and I don't think anyone else at NASA did, either.

Then it was Philip Cooney's turn:

REP. HENRY WAXMAN: It's clear from documents that the committee has received that you played a major role in reviewing and editing scientific reports about climate change. And I want to begin my questioning by asking about your qualifications for editing scientific reports. My understanding is that you're not a scientist; that you're a lawyer by training with an undergraduate degree in politics and economics. Is that correct?

PHILIP COONEY: That is correct.

WAXMAN: And prior to your move to the White House in 2001, you worked for more than 15 years at the American Petroleum Institute. Is that correct?

COONEY: That's correct.

WAXMAN: The American Petroleum Institute, or API, is the primary trade association for the oil industry, isn't it, and they're essentially lobbyists for the oil industry, aren't they?

COONEY: That's a fair characterization, yes.

WAXMAN: My understanding is that your last position with the American Petroleum Institute was as team leader of the climate team. Climate change was a major issue for the Petroleum Institute, and they were very concerned about this whole matter from an economic point of view.

While you were at the Petroleum Institute, the Petroleum Institute prepared an internal document entitled "Strategic Issues: Climate Change." . . . According to this document, and I quote, "Climate is at the center of industry's business interests. Policies limiting carbon emissions reduce petroleum product use. That is why it is API's highest-priority issue and defined as strategic."

One of the key strategies used by the Petroleum Institute was to sow doubt about climate change science. Member companies and spokesmen for the Petroleum Institute regularly exaggerated the degrees of scientific uncertainty and downplayed the role of humans in causing climate change.

What bothers me is that you seem to bring exactly the same approach inside the White House. And I want to ask you about that. We received hundreds of edits that you and your staff at the White House Council on Environmental Quality made to federal climate change reports. And there seem to be consistent reports that these edits, they exaggerate uncertainties and downplay the contribution that human activities like burning petroleum products play in causing climate change.

So when I look at the role you played at the American Petroleum Institute and then the role you played at the White House, they seem virtually identical: In both places, you were sowing doubt about the science on global warming.

COONEY: . . . Well, I think we surely were opposed to the Kyoto Protocol. But I do think that in many cases, our scientists tried to participate responsibly in some of the public dialogue that was going on and to offer legitimate views that weren't merely about sowing uncertainty as you described.

WAXMAN: My staff released an analysis of hundreds of changes that you and your staff made to federal scientific reports. Where the draft report said that climate change *will* cause adverse impacts, you changed the text to say that these changes *may* occur.

Where the draft report said that the climate change *would* damage the environment, you inserted the qualifier *potentially*.

Where the report described adverse economic effects, you modify the text to say that the economic effects could be positive or negative.

Mr. Cooney, aren't the edits you were making exactly the types of changes the Petroleum Institute itself would have made to these reports?

COONEY: . . . The comments that you're describing . . . relied on the major findings of the National Academy of Sciences according to the report that it released for the president in June 2001. And it talked about many of the localized and regionalized impacts of climate change being very poorly understood and of the inability of climate change models to project impacts at a localized and regional level.

WAXMAN: Mr. Cooney, as I understand it, every time the National Academy of Sciences has had certainty, you tried to delete that certainty or change it so that it was uncertain.

Mr. Hansen, you're one of the nation's leading experts on climate change. What's your view of the changes made by Mr. Cooney and his staff at the White House?

HANSEN: I believe that these edits—the nature of these edits is a good part of the reason for why there is a substantial gap between the understanding of global warming by the relevant scientific community and the knowledge of the public and policymakers, because there has been so much doubt cast on our understanding that they think it's still completely up in the air.

WAXMAN: Do you think the edits raise doubt where there was a consensus?

HANSEN: They consistently are always of one nature, and that is to raise doubt. Of course, there are many details about climate that remain to be understood, but that doesn't mean that we don't have a broad understanding.

WAXMAN: In a 1998 document from the Petroleum Institute that's called "Global Climate Science Communications Action Plan," . . . it says, "Victory will be achieved when average citizens understand uncertainties in climate science, recognition of uncertainties becomes part of the conventional wisdom, and media coverage reflects balance on climate science and recognition of the validity of viewpoints that challenge the current conventional wisdom."

So, when I compare this Petroleum Institute document with your activities at the White House, Mr. Cooney, I find it's hard to see much of a distinction. The Petroleum Institute defined victory as sowing doubt in the public about the certainty of climate change science. And that's what your edits to federal climate change reports appear to do.

COONEY: Mr. Chairman, . . . the National Academy [of Sciences] report . . . was our foundational document for reviewing these budgetary reports. It had truly nothing to do with my prior employment at the American Petroleum Institute.

When I came to the White House, my loyalties—my sole loyalties—were to the president and his administration.

WAXMAN: . . . Let me just point out, while my time has expired, that the points where you raised uncertainty were the places where the National Academy of Sciences were fairly certain; and the other parts where they were uncertain—I don't think that was affected.

Questioning continued by Rep. Peter Welch, a freshman Democrat from Vermont:

REP. PETER WELCH: Mr. Cooney, you indicated in your statement that your loyalty was to the president who appointed you, correct?

COONEY: Correct.

WELCH: You also indicated that your responsibility was to align the executive branch reports with administration policy, correct?

COONEY: Correct.

WELCH: And the administration had a pretty clear energy policy during the time of the ongoing energy crisis, which included recovery and the search for new oil and petroleum products, correct?

COONEY: It included that and there were many other elements.

WELCH: Well, it included supporting drilling in the Arctic National Wildlife Reserve, correct?

COONEY: It did. It included . . .

WELCH: It included drilling offshore, correct?

COONEY: I don't recall specifically.

WELCH: It included maintaining royalty relief for the oil companies for the recovery of Gulf oil even as the price of oil increased over $60 a barrel.

COONEY: I don't recall that that was an element of the national energy policy in 2001.

WELCH: It included supporting tax breaks that Congress gave the oil industry at a time when they had $125 billion in profits, correct?

COONEY: Congressman, I can say that later in my years in the administration, we opposed oil and tax—excuse me, tax incentives for oil and gas exploration for the oil industry.

WELCH: Let's get real here, Mr. Cooney, let's get real. . . . ANWR, offshore drilling, tax breaks—all advocated publicly, aggressively by the Bush administration, passed by a Republican Congress, yes or no?

COONEY: That was an element.

WELCH: Is that a hard question?

COONEY: . . . There were many elements of the policy— the promotion of nuclear energy, the increase in fuel economy standards for light trucks, a mandate for renewable fuels in the sale of transportation fuels for ethanol which was enacted in 2005—that were not necessarily to the advantage of the oil and gas industry which were administration policies.

WELCH: Let's make this simple: Did that policy of the Bush administration—and you supported the president and his policies—include promoting drilling in ANWR?

COONEY: Yes, Congressman.

WELCH: All right. Did it include support for tax breaks that were passed by Congress for the oil industry?

COONEY: I don't recall that being an element.

WELCH: ... When we examined your edits, we found a large number of changes that very clearly have the effect of emphasizing or exaggerating the level of uncertainty surrounding global warming science. In your first round of edits there were 47 edits that introduced additional uncertainty. In the second round you made 28 edits that made global warming seem less certain. And in your third round of edits you made 106 changes that introduced additional uncertainty. That's a total of 181 edits. . . .

You did have a foundation, and it was admirable loyalty to the person who had appointed you to a political position.

You know, one of the questions I have as I listen to this, whether you call it a recommendation or an edit, we'll let the people of America decide that. You described candidly that your job was to align executive reports to administration policy. Administration policy was pro-oil, pro-drilling, pro-API. As the API report said, its goal was to create uncertainty about the basis of global warming.

How is what the Petroleum Institute was doing and these edits were encouraging any different than the work of the so-called scientists during the whole tobacco debate when they were sowing doubt about whether there was any link between tobacco and lung cancer?

COONEY: Congressman, I would say that the most material development was that the president's climate change committee—Cabinet-level committee—itself requested our latest knowledge, the most current knowledge on the state of what we know about climate change at the National Academy of Sciences. That report was delivered to the Cabinet in early June 2001 and became the explicit basis for President Bush's stated policies in June 2001.

Rep. John Yarmuth (D-Ky.) questioned Philip Cooney about his edits on two major Environmental Protection Agency reports, one on the environment and the other an annual report to Congress on the changing planet:

REP. JOHN YARMUTH: You have said on numerous occasions today that you used as the basis for your editing the National Academy of Sciences and National Resource Council [NRC] documentation. . . . You talked about this being your guiding document.

Will you read the first sentence of the National Academy report aloud, please?

COONEY: "Greenhouse gases are accumulating in the Earth's atmosphere as a result of human activities causing surface air temperatures and subsurface ocean temperatures to rise."

YARMUTH: Thank you. Now please turn to exhibit B. And this is your handwritten edits to the EPA report. Now, on page 3, beginning on line 24, you've deleted a sentence from the EPA text. Will you please read that sentence aloud?

COONEY: "The NRC concluded that greenhouse gases are accumulating in the atmosphere as a result of human activities causing surface air temperatures and subsurface temperatures to rise."

YARMUTH: Right. Now, you replaced this verbatim quote from the National Academy of Sciences with your own sentence. This sentence reads, "Some activities emit greenhouse gases and other substances that directly or indirectly may affect the balance of incoming and outgoing radiation, thereby potentially affecting climate on regional and global scales."

That sentence does not appear on the academy's report. So you deleted a direct quote from the academy report, which you say is what you relied upon, and replaced it with a sentence that appears designed to obfuscate the simple reality that human activities are warming the planet. Why did you make the change and why did you not rely on the NRC report in that situation?

COONEY: . . . In this case, I don't recognize the source of the comment that I am inserting here on this draft. I don't know that it is not in the National Academy of Sciences report. I just can't say that it is.

Rep. Darrell Issa (R-Calif.) pressed Hansen about how he had described the Bush administration's effort to silence him.

ISSA: . . . Are you aware that Dr. Hansen has called the Bush administration press office the "office of propaganda," or, "It seems more like Nazi Germany or the Soviet Union than the United States"? . . . Dr. Hansen, are those kind of comments appropriate for somebody who has been on the federal payroll, who's had your science paid for, for three decades? Are those appropriate things to say about the Bush administration?

HANSEN: I think that that was in reference to the fact that scientists were being asked . . . to tell reporters, "I can't speak to you, I have to get permission, and I have to get someone on the phone with me to listen in on the conversation." That's getting to seem a lot like the—

ISSA: I think the reference to Nazi Germany, because they want to have somebody who's able to say that the doctor did or didn't say this to a reporter when it later comes out in print, is that Nazi Germany? Nazi Germany I think is a pretty strong statement, wouldn't you say?

HANSEN: I was referring to the constraints on speaking to the media. And, frankly, it violates the Constitution, freedom of speech.

ISSA: . . . But Dr. Hansen, first of all, when you work for somebody, the question of when you will speak on behalf of that entity is not a constitutional question, as you and I both know. You were not being asked by Public Broadcasting because you happen to be a smart guy with a good suit. You were being asked because of your position at NASA. Now, I come back to this again—

HANSEN: I don't think that's the case. . . . I'm an American. And I exercise my right of free speech. And if public affairs people tell me I can't do that and I know that they're violating the Constitution, I ignore them.

ISSA: But, Dr. Hansen, isn't it true that when you speak, you're speaking on federal paid time; when you travel, you're being paid by the federal government to travel? Isn't that true?

HANSEN:. . . That's exactly the point. I should be able, for the sake of the taxpayers—they should be availed of my expertise. I shouldn't be required to parrot some company line. I should give the best information that I have.

. . . When you tell scientists that they can't speak, . . . it doesn't ring true. It's not the American way. And it is not constitutional.

In spite of its public shaming, the Bush administration is determined to keep the public in the dark about global warming. In October 2007, Dr. Julie Gerberding, head of the Centers for Disease Control, was to testify in the U.S. Senate about the public health impacts of climate change. After submitting a draft of her prepared remarks to the White House Office of Management and Budget for review, her testimony "was eviscerated," according to a CDC official, shrinking from about fourteen pages to six. Gone from her remarks was information about how climate change will promote the spread of certain diseases.

White House press secretary Dana Perino defended the heavy-handed censorship. Preferring happy talk to a serious discussion about global warming, she said that the White House wanted the CDC "to focus that testimony on public health benefits. There are public health benefits to climate change, as well."[14]

The censorship came days after President Bush's top science advisor said increased global warming had no effect on natural disasters. White House Office of Science and Technology policy director John Marburger was explaining his dismissal of the widely shared target of preventing the earth's temperature from rising more than 3.6 degrees Fahrenheit. That goal, he said, "is going to be a very difficult one to achieve and is not actually linked to regional events that affect people's lives."[15]

Temperatures are rising everywhere but in the scientific never-never land of the Bush administration. It has been left to grassroots activists to turn up the political heat to a level that can't be ignored.

Turning Up the Heat

The rebellious scientists have been emboldened by worldwide movement against global warming. Activists are stepping up their efforts as the environmental crisis deepens: Arctic ice receded farther in the summer of 2007 than at any time in history, and the UN emergency relief coordinator warned in October 2007 that the world had seen a record number of floods, droughts, and storms caused by climate change already that year.

In April 2007, author and activist Bill McKibben spearheaded a remarkable national convergence called Step It Up Day. He began the effort with a half dozen students at Middlebury College in Vermont in the fall of 2006.

McKibben, who has sounded the alarm about climate change since his seminal 1989 book, *The End of Nature,* was despondent about the lack of activism on global warming. Step It Up Day called for an 80 percent reduction in carbon emissions by 2050, an immediate moratorium on new coal-fired power, and a Green Jobs for All campaign.

"We had no money and no organization, so we figured we'd be doing well if we could organize a hundred of these things by April 14. And that would have been about a hundred more global warming rallies than there had been," he told *Democracy Now!* Instead, McKibben tapped a rich vein of discontent around the United States. "People were really eager to finally be able to take action about this," said the amazed activist, "and the thing has just kinda exploded." More than fourteen hundred Step It Up rallies took place in all fifty states in April 2007. McKibben followed with another Step It Up Day seven months later, which involved hundreds of thousands of people around the country, including eighty members of Congress.

Ted Glick, coordinator of the U.S. Climate Emergency Council, helped organize a "No War, No Warming" nonviolent civil disobedience action on Capitol Hill in October 2007. Sixty-one people, some of them in polar bear costumes, were arrested as some blocked a street to protest the wars in Iraq and Afghanistan and the Bush administration's record on climate change. Glick had begun a fast in September 2007 to protest the failure of lawmakers in Washington to address climate change. "There is no sense of urgency about the climate crisis," Glick told *Democracy Now!* in October 2007 just after President Bush had blown off an international climate summit at the UN. By late October, the fasting activist had lost thirty-five pounds. "So there is a need for, quite frankly, more extreme actions."

A broad coalition of groups, ranging from Greenpeace to the Sierra Club and the Union of Concerned Scientists, has taken aim at ExxonMobil, the piggy bank of the global warming denial movement. The Exxpose Exxon campaign has succeeded in mobilizing Congress and educating the public about Exxon's role in supporting junk science and "keeping America addicted to oil." This public shaming resulted in Exxon-funded climate denier groups losing more than $1.4 million in 2006, or nearly 40 percent of their funding from the oil giant compared to the year before.[16]

Just like prospecting for black gold, the oil industry is finding new ways to influence science and public discourse. It hit a gusher when it started to buy off universities. ExxonMobil has given $100 million to Stanford University to help establish the Global Climate and Energy Project (GCEP). The program, founded in 2002, is cosponsored by Toyota ($50 million), General Electric ($50 million), and Schlumberger ($25 million), an oilfield services company. While the GCEP claims to be focused on researching low-emissions energy technologies, Exxon wasted little time in hitching Stanford's name to its agenda. In an Exxon ad that ran on the op-ed page of the *New York Times,* the oil company crowed about its partnership with the "best minds" at Stanford.

The ad declared that "there is a lively debate about . . . the climate's response to the presence of more greenhouse gases in the atmosphere." But there was a new twist: The ad was signed by Franklin M. Orr, Jr., the professor who heads GCEP, and it included the Stanford seal. This occurred while ExxonMobil was fighting off laws that might require mandatory greenhouse gas reduction; instead, Exxon called for more research. And here was Stanford, providing the research—and the perfect cover.[17]

Exxon is not alone. BP announced in February 2007 that it was investing $500 million over ten years in a biofuels research program at UC Berkeley, in collaboration with Lawrence Berkeley Livermore Labs and the University of Illinois. BP will have fifty of its own scientists working alongside academicians and will gain limited exclusive commercial licenses from some research. With the university now awash in BP's money, the oil company will have an unprecedented ability to set the agenda at the once public university.

UC President Robert Dynes acknowledged that the money will fundamentally change Berkeley. "It is my belief," he said, "that we are reinventing the research university in this public-private partnership."[18]

The Berkeley deal has met with protest from faculty and students, who dub the university "BPerkeley." Anthropology professor Laura Nader said at a protest in October 2007 that she came to Berkeley "to teach at a public university, not a corporatized university," while biology professor Miguel Altieri charged that biofuels will destroy food-growing land, resulting in higher food prices and hunger.[19]

"For a mere $50 million a year," wrote Jennifer Washburn in the *Los Angeles Times* about the BP-Berkeley deal, "an oil company worth $250 billion would buy a chunk of America's premier public research institutions, all but turning them into its own profit-making subsidiary."[20]

Environmentalist Paul Ehrlich, a Stanford professor, mused on *Democracy Now!*, "Some money is so dirty you can't really wash it."[21]

Oil company apologists don't appreciate having these messy realities exposed. George Shultz, secretary of state under President Reagan, former head of Bechtel Corporation, and a close confidant of the Bush family, spoke at a panel on energy at Stanford in September 2007 that Amy moderated. Shultz, who now claims to be a newly minted, Prius-driving global warming activist, was discussing China. Amy asked, "Who do you think is tougher to get on board on taking global warming seriously: China or Exxon-Mobil?"

Visibly irritated by the question, Shultz replied, "I'm not going to bite on that. Thank you very much. And that's enough." He then pulled off his mike.

The awarding of the Nobel Peace Prize to former vice president Al Gore and the Intergovernmental Panel on Climate Change in December 2007 is a clear sign that global warming activism has forced the issue to the front of the international agenda. From Step It Up marches to international treaties, the climate change movement continues to reinvent itself. Scientists have been vindicated. Activists are energized.

As Al Gore said in accepting the Nobel Peace Prize, "The future is knocking at our door right now. . . . The next generation will ask us one of two questions. Either they will ask: 'What were you thinking; why didn't you act?' Or they will ask instead: 'How did you find the moral courage to rise and successfully resolve a crisis that so many said was impossible to solve?'

"We have everything we need to get started, save perhaps political will, but political will is a renewable resource. So let us renew it, and say together: 'We have a purpose. We are many. For this purpose we will rise, and we will act.'"

CHAPTER 5

Psychologists in Denial

Jean Maria Arrigo stood on the dais before the standing-room-only crowd of hundreds of psychologists. The scene was the annual convention of the American Psychological Association (APA) in San Francisco in August 2007. A shock of short gray hair framed her face, and a faint smile was fixed on her jaw. Beside her sat some of the top brass of her professional organization. She knew them all, since she had served with them on an APA task force in 2005 that examined the role played by psychologists in national security interrogations.

The task force had been formed in response to critics, including many APA members, who charged that psychologists were participating in or aiding torture in military detention centers such as at Guantánamo Bay, Cuba, and Bagram Air Base, Afghanistan, and at secret CIA prisons overseas known as "black sites." But the APA task force had concluded that psychologists working in interrogations play "a valuable and ethical role." Now this petite woman was about to deliver a body blow to her former task force members, publicly exposing some of them and their ties to torture.

Jean Maria Arrigo is an improbable heroine. A shy, bookish, and slightly awkward social psychologist who specializes in oral histories of military intelligence officers, she was little known outside her arcane area of interest. So she was surprised when then APA president Ron Levant asked her to join the APA Presidential Task Force on Psychological Ethics and National Security (PENS). "I was nobody," she told us as we talked with her at her San Francisco hotel one evening during the APA convention. She was disarmingly candid, at times telling us more about her life than we wanted to know. But she was also sharply perceptive about what happened when she unwittingly stumbled into the shadowy world of terrorists, interrogation, and torture centers.

"I became a psychologist at 54, so I was a relatively safe person" for APA officials to choose, she said. "And they knew I did this work with the military, so maybe they thought I'd fall into line. Of all the people they could have picked, I was the least threatening."

When the PENS task force convened at APA headquarters in Washington, D.C., in June 2005, Arrigo began to sense that something was not right. First, the meeting was shrouded in secrecy, and members were told not to speak to the press and to refer all media inquiries to APA officials. Arrigo asked whether the task force would be investigating what psychologists were doing at Guantánamo Bay. It was the obvious question: Didn't the APA want to know what was being done in the name of psychology in America's most notorious interrogation center? She says that incoming APA president Gerald Koocher, supposedly there only as a liaison to the APA board, dismissed the idea and "really laid into me. He said, 'If you don't like the constraints of the task force, you should have stayed home.'"

When Arrigo began jotting down notes, Scott Shumate, another task force member, ordered her to stop. "It makes me very uncomfortable when there is someone in the room taking notes," she recalls him snapping at her. Arrigo, who describes herself as "a compulsive note taker," did not reply, and discreetly continued what she was doing. Shumate, she would later learn, had a reason to fear someone documenting his work: He was an "operational psychologist" for the CIA.

A few hours after the task force convened, APA officials distributed a draft of the report that the participants were to issue. Arrigo was shocked they had written it so fast. The whole process appeared to be rigged: The task force could debate and modify the draft, but the parameters of the discussion and key conclusions had been predetermined. The task force met for the weekend, and its report was then rushed to the APA board of directors for emergency approval. One week later, the PENS report, which mysteriously did not include the names of any of the task force members, was released. The study was swiftly hailed by the APA as "a thorough and thoughtful report." Critics dismissed it as a whitewash that gave cover to torturers.

Arrigo was deeply disturbed by the secrecy that surrounded the PENS task force and its report. She knew something was wrong; she just couldn't put her finger on what it was. Then in July 2006, reporter Mark Benjamin revealed in Salon.com that six of the nine voting members of the task force worked in or closely with the military or the CIA. Several of them held command positions for psychologists in places where psychologist abuses had been reported. The APA had withheld the names and backgrounds of the PENS members from the public, but Benjamin had obtained them from congressional sources.

In other words, the APA had asked psychologists who were potentially implicated in abuses to sit in judgment of themselves.

So when Arrigo rose to speak at the APA convention in 2007, it was not to hail her work on the APA task force, but to pull back the curtain on the shocking story of how the world's largest organization of psychologists had become an apologist for torture.

"I stand before you a very miserable person," she began, in the tensely quiet room. "I wish I weren't here, because many of the people on the task force I actually liked better than some of my close friends. But, you know, here's how it [goes]."

Arrigo told the audience that APA president Gerald Koocher "represented the PENS report as the product of an independent ten-member task force. I knew it was not independent."

Which has left everyone wondering: Who are the psychologists covering for, and why?

Psychologists in Denial

Torture? Protesting psychologists? Is this the punch line to some kind of Freudian joke? To prisoners at Guantánamo Bay and secret CIA prisons, it is more like a nightmare: Psychologists now stand alone among major health care providers in being willing to participate in interrogations at military and CIA facilities. Now there is the threat that psychologists could be prosecuted for war crimes.

Despite a stream of revelations about the central role that psychologists have played in the torture of alleged terrorist prisoners, the 148,000-member American Psychological Association has fought off calls both from within and outside its ranks to pull out of America's most notorious torture centers.

In 2006, the American Psychiatric Association and the American Medical Association both barred their members from taking part in military interrogations. Even the Society for Ethnomusicology has taken a stand against torture, in response to reports that the U.S. military has used blaring music to torment prisoners at Abu Ghraib and Guantánamo.

Psychologists are now "the last ones willing to do this dirty work," charged Steven Reisner, PhD, a psychoanalyst who is on the faculty at Columbia and New York University. He began working closely with Arrigo in 2006 and is now a leader of a growing group of dissident psychologists, the Coalition for Ethical Psychology, who are demanding that the APA declare a moratorium on psychologist participation in all military and CIA interrogations.

The issue came to a head at the 2007 APA annual convention. After days of late-night negotiations, the moratorium came up for a climactic vote. We saw a surreal scene on the convention floor: Uniformed military were out in force. Men and women in desert camo and navy whites worked the APA Council of Representatives, and officers in crisp dress uniforms stepped to the microphones.

Military psychologists insisted that they help make interrogations safe, ethical, and legal, and cited instances where psychologists allegedly intervened to stop abuse. "If we remove psychologists from these facilities, people are going to die!" boomed Col. Larry James of the U.S. Army, chief psychologist at Guantánamo Bay and a member of the APA governing body.

Why are people dying if the U.S. military is in charge? Dr. Laurie Wagner, a Dallas psychologist and the past president of the APA Division of Psychoanalysis, shot back, "If psychologists have to be there in order to keep detainees from being killed, then those conditions are so horrendous that the only moral and ethical thing to do is to protest by leaving."

Moments later, the APA Council of Representatives rejected a measure banning association members from participating in any interrogations at detention centers. Instead, it passed a resolution condemning "torture and cruel, inhuman, or degrading treatment or punishment," and prohibiting psychologists from participating in nineteen specific techniques, such as mock executions, rape, waterboarding, or physical assault. But some techniques, such as isolation and sleep deprivation, were barred only when "used in a manner that represents significant pain or suffering or in a manner that a reasonable person would judge to cause lasting harm." This caveat is cryptic—and crucial, since it appears to leave room for "enhanced interrogation" techniques authorized by President Bush in July 2007 for use at CIA black sites. Bush has been determined to allow the CIA to torture, and the APA appeared to be going along.

Boston psychoanalyst Stephen Soldz, an organizer of the interrogation moratorium, was outraged. He told us that "do no harm" is part of the Hippocratic oath taken by physicians, and is a cardinal principle of psychology. "By endorsing that it is an ethical thing for psychologists to do harm as long as it doesn't cause 'significant pain and suffering and long-lasting impairment'—this is a very sad day for psychology."

Tortured Logic

The world's leading human rights groups, ~~from~~ ~~Red~~ Cross to Amnesty International to the United ~~Nations~~ denounced as torture the interrogation tactics ~~used at Guan~~tánamo Bay where some 300 prisoners were being held in late 2007, and at the super-secret foreign black sites where the CIA has kept a number of "high-value" prisoners. In addition to these prisons, the United States is holding nearly 25,000 people in prisons in Iraq.[1]

American-style torture differs from the medieval torments such as fingernail-pulling and whipping. The CIA and the military discovered through human experiments in the fifties and sixties that psychological torture was far more destructive than physical torture. Severe mental anguish, went the thinking, would force prisoners to divulge useful information.

Professor Alfred McCoy at the University of Wisconsin-Madison, who has written a history of CIA interrogation tactics, explained on *Democracy Now!*, "If you look at the most famous of photographs from Abu Ghraib—of the Iraqi standing on the box, arms extended with a hood over his head and the fake electrical wires from his arms—in that photograph you can see the entire fifty-year history of CIA torture. It's very simple: He's hooded for sensory disorientation, and his arms are extended for self-inflicted pain. Those are the two very simple fundamental CIA techniques, developed at enormous cost."

The CIA codified its findings in 1963 in the KUBARK Counterintelligence Manual. McCoy noted that KUBARK ted "a distinctively American form of torture, the first revolution in the cruel science of pain in centuries: psychological torture. . . . It's proved to be a very resilient, quite adaptable, and an enormously destructive paradigm."[2]

The CIA and the U.S. military need psychologists in order to effectively inflict psychological torture. The role that psychologists played in devising and implementing interrogations at Guantánamo Bay (a.k.a. Gitmo) became clearer in May 2007 following the release of a previously classified report by the Pentagon inspector general. The report revealed that military psychologists oversaw the adaptation of the military's Survive, Evade, Resist, and Escape (SERE) program for use against prisoners in "terror" interrogations. SERE was originally designed to train U.S. troops to resist the torture techniques once used by Soviet and Chinese interrogators to extract false confessions. SERE training is intended "to replicate harsh conditions that the service member might encounter if they are held by forces that do not abide by the Geneva Conventions."[3] By using SERE techniques against prisoners, the United States has become the country that is violating the Geneva Conventions.

Psychologists play a central role in SERE training, which includes enduring stress positions, sleep deprivation, hooding, isolation, starvation, sexual humiliation, forced nudity, and more—exactly the techniques used against prisoners at Guantánamo and Abu Ghraib. This is no coincidence: SERE psychologists helped train Guantánamo interrogators and members of its Behavioral Science Consultation Teams (BSCT—or "biscuit") to "reverse-engineer" the SERE techniques for use against prisoners. In a rare leaked report, the International Committee of the Red Cross described in 2004 how Guantánamo had implemented "an intentional system of cruel, unusual and degrading treatment and a form of torture." The Red Cross said that it was BSCT members, including psychologists, who conveyed information to interrogators about detainee "mental health and vulnerabilities" to help break down prisoners.[4]

This torture regimen was outlined in the standard operating procedures manual for Guantánamo Bay in 2003; the document was leaked on the Internet in late 2007. The manual revealed how new prisoners were to be kept in isolation—and hidden from Red Cross investigators, in violation of the Geneva Conventions—for their first month, in order to "enhance and exploit the disorientation and disorganization felt by a newly arrived detainee in the interrogation process." This process of sensory deprivation and isolation, which was overseen by psychologists, is the time-tested psychological torture program devised and used by the U.S. military and the CIA.

The brutality of SERE techniques was in evidence in the interrogation of Mohammed al-Qahtani, believed by some to be the missing twentieth hijacker of the 9/11 attacks. Secret interrogation logs obtained by *Time* in 2005 detailed how, from November 2002 to January 2003, interrogators at Guantánamo experimented with ways to torment al-Qahtani into confessing. His torture, which was directly authorized by Secretary of Defense Donald Rumsfeld, included forcing him to urinate on himself, months of isolation, sleep deprivation, and blaring loud music, even when he was in the hospital. "They strip-search him and briefly make him stand nude," the interrogation log recounts matter-of-factly. "They tell him to bark like a dog and growl at pictures of terrorists.

They hang pictures of scantily clad women around his neck. A female interrogator so annoys al-Qahtani [she was performing lap dances on him] that he tells his captors he wants to commit suicide and asks for a crayon to write a will."[5] According to *The New England Journal of Medicine,* the first BSCT psychologist, Major John Leso, attended al-Qahtani's interrogation.[6]

An FBI agent witnessed some of the abuses and objected to the Pentagon that al-Qahtani had been "subjected to intense isolation for over three months" and "was evidencing behavior consistent with extreme psychological trauma (talking to nonexistent people, reporting hearing voices, crouching in a cell covered with a sheet for hours on end)."[7] No one was ever held accountable for the abuse.

This is psychology, Gitmo-style. In the secrecy of an offshore prison, torture is immaculately conceived: No one ordered it. No one saw it. And no one tortured.

So President Bush can say with a straight face to the world—and a wink to the torturers—"America does not torture." And APA psychologists give him the cover he desperately needs.

Guantánamo interrogation tactics were swiftly exported to detention centers in Iraq and Afghanistan. In 2003, Maj. Gen. Geoffrey Miller, the head of the Guantánamo Bay prison, was dispatched by Rumsfeld to Iraq's Abu Ghraib prison. Miller famously vowed to "Gitmo-ize" Abu Ghraib. He delivered on his promise.

When the photos of horrific abuses at Abu Ghraib leaked out in 2004, there was a public outcry. In response, Sen. John McCain, who was himself tortured as a prisoner of war in Vietnam, sponsored the Detainee Treatment Act of 2005, which was an attempt to bar torture. But when President Bush signed the law, he attached an unusual "signing statement," reserving the right to ignore the law. So torture continues unabated.

Legality and ethics notwithstanding, torture is disastrously ineffective. Prisoners will say anything to stop their abuse, so there has been little useful intelligence gleaned from the torture sessions. Which is exactly what happened with the Pentagon's trophy prisoner, Mohammed al-Qahtani. He ultimately "confessed" in June 2005, claiming that thirty other Guantánamo prisoners were Osama bin Laden's bodyguards. The Pentagon claimed that this was vital intelligence. A year later, al-Qahtani repudiated all his confessions, claiming that they were extracted under torture.[8] Military prosecutors said that what had been done to him would prevent him from ever being put on trial.[9] This helps explain why, by early 2008, no prisoners at Guantánamo Bay have had trials, despite spending up to six years or more in captivity.

Psychologists have been at the center of some of the most sadistic interrogations. Two CIA-contracted psychologists, James Elmer Mitchell and Bruce Jessen, designed the torture tactics used on detainees held in secret CIA black sites. Both were SERE psychologists and helped to reverse-engineer the SERE tactics to inflict on prisoners. The CIA put them in charge of training interrogators in the brutal techniques, including "waterboarding," at its network of black sites. Mitchell was present at the interrogation of al-Qaeda lieutenant Abu Zubaydah in a CIA safe house in Thailand. Reporter Katherine Eban, who wrote about the incident for vanityfair.com, told *Democracy Now!*, "Mitchell showed up at the safe house, along with the chief psychologist for the counterterrorism center, Dr. R. Scott Shumate, who, I should mention, was a member of the APA's task force on interrogation policy. Mitchell said that 'We're going to use these harsh interrogation tactics in order to extract all the possible information from Zubaydah.' And among those was a coffin in which they were planning to bury him alive. . . . Shumate protested the tactics and subsequently told associates, as we had learned, that he thought it was a mistake for the CIA to hire contractors.

"Nonetheless, at the time, Mitchell said that the interrogators were going to be Zubaydah's god and that they would basically bestow privileges or take them away, depending on his level of cooperation. And basically his philosophy . . . is to completely break down a detainee through white noise, through complete separation of his personality, to completely unmoor him and make him completely dependent on his interrogators. And it was through that psychic breakdown he had planned to extract as much intelligence as possible."[10]

Their company, Mitchell, Jessen & Associates, is "booming," said Eban. They reportedly have 120 employees in their offices in Spokane, Washington, and are paid more than $1,000 per day for their services. Mitchell and Jessen issued a statement in response to questions from vanityfair.com saying, "We are proud of the work we have done for our country."[11]

In December 2007, the *New York Times* revealed that the CIA had secretly destroyed videotapes of two interrogations. One of them was the interrogation of Abu Zubaydah. It is widely suspected that the CIA was trying to protect its agents—including its psychologists—from charges that they had participated in war crimes.

A group of World War II interrogators who gathered for a

reunion in October 2007 recalled interrogations that did work. "We got more information out of a German general with a game of chess or Ping-Pong than they do today, with their torture," said Henry Kolm, 90, an MIT physicist who had been assigned to play chess in Germany with Hitler's deputy, Rudolf Hess.

"During the many interrogations, I never laid hands on anyone," said George Frenkel, 87, of Maryland. "We extracted information in a battle of the wits. I'm proud to say I never compromised my humanity."[12]

In 2007, a seemingly strange, but telling, sequence of events occurred. In July 2007, President Bush signed an executive order permitting the use of "enhanced interrogation" techniques by the CIA, which included waterboarding (drowning). In August, the APA passed its resolution condemning torture. But it, too, left room for psychologists to work at CIA black sites, where enhanced interrogations take place. Then in October 2007, the *New York Times* revealed the existence of secret Justice Department memos that offered "an expansive endorsement of the harshest interrogation techniques ever used by the Central Intelligence Agency." Despite President Bush's public assurances to the contrary, the secret legal opinions "for the first time provided explicit authorization to barrage terror suspects with a combination of painful physical and psychological tactics, including head-slapping, simulated drowning and frigid temperatures."[13]

So while President Bush was providing legal cover to enable the CIA to torture, the APA was offering professional cover to enable psychologists working with the CIA to participate in harsh interrogations.

Is "enhanced interrogation" torture? A damning answer came from a surprising corner: conservative, pro-war pundit Andrew Sullivan. His scathing dissent is a sign of how a revulsion against torture has united people across the political spectrum. Sullivan wrote in the *Times* of London:

> One way to answer this question is to examine history. The phrase ["enhanced interrogation"] has a lineage. *Verschärfte Vernehmung,* enhanced or intensified interrogation, was the exact term innovated by the Gestapo to describe what became known as the "third degree." It left no marks. It included hypothermia, stress positions and long-time sleep deprivation.
>
> The United States prosecuted it as a war crime in Norway in 1948. The victims were not in uniform—they were part of the Norwegian insurgency against the German occupation—and the Nazis argued, just as Cheney has done, that this put them outside base-line protections (subsequently formalized by the Geneva conventions).[14]

President George W. Bush and Vice President Dick Cheney have at last bestowed an American seal of approval on these long-reviled Nazi interrogation tactics.

Hidden Agendas

Some members of the PENS task force had good reason to want cover. Col. Morgan Banks, a task force member, was the chief SERE psychologist for the army; he advised BSCT teams at Guantánamo and at Bagram Air Base in Afghanistan.[15] A June 2007 letter to APA president Sharon Brehm, signed by more than 750 APA members, charged, "Colonel Banks was intimately involved in the teaching and development of the abusive interrogation tactics documented by the International Committee of the Red Cross, and now by the Department of Defense, as being used at Guantánamo."[16]

Another PENS task force member was Capt. Bryce Lefever. He is a SERE psychologist whose APA bio describes him as having supervised "personnel undergoing intensive exposure to enemy interrogation, torture, and exploitation techniques"—the very techniques employed against prisoners in American custody.[17]

Then there was Col. Larry James, who spoke so forcefully against the APA interrogation moratorium in 2007. He was chief psychologist at Guántanamo in 2003 and was also the first psychologist at Abu Ghraib in 2004, periods when serious human rights violations occurred in those interrogation centers.[18]

Finally, there was Scott Shumate, the man who tried to prevent Jean Maria Arrigo from taking notes. As the chief operational psychologist for the CIA's Counter Terrorism Center, from 2001 to 2003, according to his APA bio, he "has interviewed many renowned individuals associated with various terrorist networks"; another bio states that Shumate "has been with several of the key apprehended terrorists including Abu Zubaydah."[19]

The letter to APA president Brehm, which had been organized by Reisner, Soldz, and Northwestern University psychologist Brad Olsen, concluded, "It is now indisputable that psychologists and psychology were directly and officially responsible for the development and migration of abusive interrogation techniques, techniques which the International

Committee of the Red Cross has labeled 'tantamount to torture.' "[20]

Col. Larry James strongly defended himself in his own open letter to APA president Brehm. "The authors of this letter—who do not know me, my values or my work—have seen fit to besmirch my reputation by associating me with the perpetration of torture." He continued, "I will be as clear as I possibly can: I strongly object to, have never used, and will never use torture, cruel, or abusive treatment or punishment of any kind, for any reason, in any setting. They are antithetical to who I am as a person and as an officer in the United States military."[21]

Defenders of the APA's position claim that psychologists are needed at interrogations to protect the prisoners and to ensure that the interrogators do not go over the line. "If we remove [psychologists] from the process, we do that at peril to our profession, and to detainees," insisted Capt. Morgan Sammons, PhD, psychology specialty leader in the navy and head of an APA division on pharmacotherapy. He spoke at one of ten sessions about torture and interrogation at the APA annual convention that we attended.

Col. Larry James added in his open letter, "APA's continuing work has given psychologists an invaluable resource to fight against ill-informed and misguided promoters of harsh and abusive interrogation techniques. *We are making excellent progress in that fight*" (emphasis in original).[22]

Steven Reisner countered, "If you have a site where detainees are kept in indefinite isolation, in indefinite confinement, without an end, without due process, then you have affected their psychology in a way that makes any interrogation an interrogation of abuse." Reisner and his colleagues dismissed Colonel James's defense. They pointed out that a year after James arrived at Guantánamo Bay, the International Committee of the Red Cross had reported that interrogations, far from becoming more humane, had become "more refined and more repressive."[23]

It is not just rank-and-file psychologists who are protesting. Former APA president Philip Zimbardo is an international expert on interrogation and torture, and the author of *The Lucifer Effect: Understanding How Good People Turn Evil.* We asked for his response to the oft-repeated argument that psychologists can protect prisoners from abuse. "I think that's a lie," he told us. "Nobody is paying psychologists to go to the prison to make life easier for the prisoners. Psychologists in operation in Guantánamo Bay, in Abu Ghraib, in Afghanistan have almost no power to make any meaningful change. They are hired guns. You do what the boss wants, or you don't get back. So to say that psychologists are needed to maintain the dignity of prisoners, their health and so forth—that has no basis in reality."

At times, the APA convention seemed to mimic the obsessive secrecy of the military. *Democracy Now!* tried to film some of the sessions but was ordered to shut off its equipment supposedly due to privacy concerns of some of the panelists who worked with the military. At a town hall meeting about interrogations that took place during the convention, APA officials threatened to call security to eject *Democracy Now!* if it did not stop filming. Amy finally took the podium and asked APA members whether they agreed to such secrecy. The psychologists, who were unaware of the media restrictions, were outraged. After tense consultations, APA leaders backed down and allowed the filming to continue.

In a surreal moment at the opening APA session on ethics and interrogations, a former Guantánamo civilian interrogator, "Dr. Katherine Sherwood" (she was using a pseudonym, and refused to identify herself to us afterward), wanted the audience to know that interrogations are conducted professionally. As proof, she described how interrogators were denied access to prisoners' medical records in an apparent effort to protect their privacy. She recounted, "I like to bake at home for the detainees and bring home-baked goods to our sessions. I needed to know whether or not a detainee had a peanut allergy, and that could be very serious. There was a process in place where . . . the liaison could ask the medical personnel, and they could choose whether or not to give a response."

Her baking gives new meaning to the term "biscuit" psychologists.

A Renegade and a Movement

As she sat through the PENS meeting at APA headquarters in Washington in 2005, Jean Maria Arrigo felt distraught, alone, and unsure what to do. She was castigated for raising questions, and received no support from other task force members. She sensed that there were other agendas being pursued by members of the task force, but she did not understand what they were. Arrigo said, "I had no status. I was not getting a paycheck. All these people have status." She called her husband and cried. He told her, "If you are this upset about it, then you should be there." Arrigo says she interpreted his advice as "stay and betray."

But how? Unbeknownst to Arrigo, an anti-torture movement was already coalescing among psychologists. The renegade and the movement needed each other.

Steven Reisner, who counsels torture victims, told us that he was motivated to act when he read in the press that children were being held at Guantánamo Bay, and some were attempting suicide. According to the International Committee of the Red Cross, military psychologists dismissed the problems as preexisting conditions. Reisner said, "It became clear that psychologists were using psychology to perpetuate the military position in the global war on terror, going against what any psychologist would say." This view was bolstered by an article in 2005 in *The New England Journal of Medicine* that reported, "Since late 2002, psychiatrists and psychologists have been part of a strategy that employs extreme stress, combined with behavior-shaping reward, to extract actionable intelligence from resistant captives."[24]

These reports, along with the ICRC assessment that health care providers at Gitmo were in "flagrant violation of medical ethics," confirmed what many psychologists suspected about the abuse. "We knew psychologists were implicated," said Reisner. Following the ICRC report on Guantánamo, Reisner decided to fight. He teamed up with Physicians for Human Rights and pressed ahead with a campaign to get the APA to unequivocally ban its members from participating in interrogations, following the lead of the American Psychiatric Association.

For Reisner, a dark-haired, bearded man who appears perpetually disheveled as he races between negotiations and late-night organizing sessions at the convention, the mission to end torture is personal: His parents were Holocaust survivors, and his father escaped from Poland to Russia, only to endure harsh interrogations there. "What the suffering of the Holocaust gives those of us who are touched by it is the requirement that we stay separate from any authority and keep attention to fighting where such things might take place on any level. I am an activist against oppression and cruelty in the name of anything."

Another psychologist who joined in the effort was Boston psychoanalyst Stephen Soldz. Through writing articles and blogging, Soldz wanted to broaden the struggle. Sitting at the APA convention in San Francisco, Soldz was intense, earnest, and committed. "I always saw the goal was to get the broader public involved. It's not a guild issue for psychologists. It's an issue of torture, which concerns the world."

Reisner had heard that Jean Maria Arrigo had serious misgivings about the PENS report. When he met her at the APA convention in 2006, she was at first reluctant to tell all about what had happened during the PENS process. "I felt kind of skittish," the math teacher turned psychologist told us. "I guess I like a sense of civility around things." But when Reisner explained how the military people on the committee had a personal stake in ensuring that the APA did not condemn the role of psychologists in interrogations, Arrigo turned. "This isn't just a little bit slippery," she said. "This is off the scale."

Arrigo realized that she had been a pawn in a carefully orchestrated effort to give cover to people who might be involved in torture—which included some of her task force colleagues. The daughter of a military interrogator, Arrigo was especially troubled. "What animates me is all these military people who wanted to do good being in these horrible situations that they can't figure how to get out of. Here we are on the outside, and we can't even stand up for them," she told us. "In a way, corrupting those military people offends me more than torturing people."

Arrigo has since thrown all her energy into exposing the APA's connection to torturers. She has withstood personal attacks from APA leaders, including a nasty open letter sent to *Democracy Now!* in August 2007 from former APA president Gerald Koocher that attempted to smear her by questioning her "personal biases and troubled past." Koocher claimed that Arrigo's "personal difficulties" stem partly from her father having "committed suicide." It was one of many bizarre distortions and attempts to discredit her: Arrigo's father is, in fact, alive and well in California.

The problem for the APA is that Arrigo is not the only member of the PENS task force who rebelled. All three voting civilian psychologists on the task force who did not have ties to the military have strongly criticized the secrecy and influence of the military on the panel. PENS task force member Dr. Nina Thomas, a faculty member at New York University, did not understand the role in interrogations played by fellow task force member Col. Morgan Banks, who was chief SERE psychologist for the army and advised Guantánamo BSCT teams. "I knew the outline of his background, but I didn't know the meaning of his background. So it disturbs me," she said on *Democracy Now!*

Dr. Michael Wessells, a psychologist and professor at both Columbia University and Randolph-Macon College, resigned in protest from the PENS task force in January 2006. Wessells charged on *Democracy Now!,* "When I got inside the [PENS meeting] room, it became clear that this was predominantly a national security establishment operation. . . . The PENS Task Force refused to speak out in a concerted manner against human rights abuses." Former APA president Gerald Koocher dismissed the Wessells resignation, claiming that the PENS task force had "expired" a month earlier.

Arrigo is undeterred by the attacks against her. In the fall of 2006, she turned over her forbidden notes and e-mails from the PENS deliberations to the Hoover Institution Archives at Stanford University for safekeeping. She also provided notes and information to Reisner, to Physicians for Human Rights, and to vanityfair.com. Finally, she turned over her notes to the Senate Armed Services Committee, which held closed-door hearings in late 2007 about the role of psychologists in interrogation. Arrigo hopes that the Senate will finally expose and help sever the ties between psychologists and torture.

In Bed with the Military

The question has baffled human rights advocates: Why has the leadership of the APA fought so hard to keep psychologists in places such as Guantánamo Bay? One psychologist who spoke out at the convention hinted at the answer, "It's like we're embedded in the military."

It turns out that APA and the military have been linked since birth. "The roots of contemporary psychology are in war and defense efforts," Steven Breckler, head of the APA science directorate, told us. Psychology as a science distinct from psychiatry (psychiatrists, who are physicians, can prescribe drugs, and psychologists cannot) came into prominence with World War II, when the U.S. military turned to psychologists for testing and evaluation of soldiers. Psychology "got a big boost" from the war, said Breckler. In the 1950s, nearly all federal funding for social science came from the military, and psychologists have been working closely with the military and intelligence agencies ever since.

Psychology was a key weapon in the Cold War. In the 1950s, Donald Hebb, a past president of the APA, and others pioneered research into isolation and sensory and sleep deprivation, which promptly became the cornerstone of CIA interrogation practice. In the decades since, countless psychologists have done their graduate work on military-funded projects; James Mulick, professor of pediatrics and psychology at Ohio State University, told us about Project Themis, an Air Force–funded program he worked on at the University of Vermont, wherein volunteers were placed into a soundproof chamber for a month at a time. "We were told this was being done to see how it affected their sense of time," Mulick says. "But we were taking both physical and psychological measurements, and I could see that it had other uses." The project's main investigator, UVM psychology chairman Donald Forgays, publicized the findings in military publications and at NATO conferences.

The APA remains umbilically connected to the Pentagon. While the number of military psychologists in the APA is small—there are only about five hundred members of the APA's Division of Military Psychology, which also includes civilians who work with the military—they have outsized influence in the organization. That's because military money talks. The APA aggressively lobbies for funding from the military services, the Department of Homeland Security, the Defense Advanced Research Projects Agency (DARPA), and the DOD Counterintelligence Field Activity (CIFA), to name a few. In fiscal year 2003, DOD spending on behavioral, cognitive, and social science research stood at about $405 million.

Critics have charged that the APA has reaped coveted professional benefits from its association with the military. In the 1990s, the Department of Defense ran a pilot program allowing psychologists to prescribe drugs, a privilege the APA has long championed. The prescribing psychologist program was launched in 1991 at the urging of Patrick DeLeon, PhD, an APA board member who served as APA president in 2000. DeLeon, a lawyer and psychologist, is a longtime aide and currently the chief of staff to Sen. Daniel Inouye (D-Hawaii), former chair of the Senate Armed Services Committee. The DOD spent $6 million on the pilot program and trained ten psychologists to prescribe drugs; the program was halted in 1997 following a report by the General Accounting Office that charged that the program was wasteful and unnecessary. Some of the prescribing military psychologists are leaders within the APA and were instrumental in blocking efforts to ban psychologists from interrogation centers.

Any suggestion that the APA has been bought off by the military is nonsense, the APA's Breckler insists. "Collaboration does not mean capitulation. We are not in bed with them."

Perhaps not in bed, but psychologists have done well at the bank. APA leaders have long occupied important positions where they receive military funding. The Human Research Resources Organization (HumRRO) was founded in 1951 by Dr. Meredith Crawford, a former APA treasurer, exclusively to do research in behavioral and social science for the U.S. Army. HumRRO, which for many years was entirely funded by the military, now gets about 55 percent of its work from the armed forces. The organization is intimately connected with the APA: The chairman of HumRRO's board is James McHugh, who is also senior counsel to the APA; vice chair Charles McCay is the APA's chief financial officer; and HumRRO vice president Bill Strickland is past president of the APA Division of Military Psychology and has been a vocal opponent of barring psychologists from military detention centers.

Other APA leaders with military ties include former APA president Joseph Matarazzo, who is a part owner and board member of Mitchell, Jessen & Associates, the Spokane-based CIA contractor that has been implicated in devising brutal interrogation techniques for the CIA.[25] Mitchell, Jessen is being investigated by the Senate Armed Services Committee.

"There are multiple vested interests" in keeping things the way they are, conceded former APA president Philip Zimbardo, who described the organization's interrogation policy as "Orwellian." He added, "There's some deeper level of complicity that we don't understand."

In their determination to be last to leave the torture centers, psychologists may wind up the first ones in the dock. A letter from the ACLU arrived at the APA conference just before the fateful vote. "The participation of psychologists in cruel, inhuman, and degrading interrogation of detainees is not only unethical but illegal, and may subject APA members to legal liability or even prosecution," wrote ACLU executive director Anthony Romero. "It is no longer enough to speak out against torture; rather we must sever the connection between healers and tormentors once and for all."

Heeding this warning will require the American Psychological Association to unembed itself from the U.S. military. Meanwhile, as APA member Dan Aalbers declared, "This detention and interrogation policy is going to go down. And once it does go down, we will find that we have secured the best cabin on the *Titanic*."

The struggle against torture continues on many fronts. Psychologists are determined to reclaim their profession and place it firmly among the healing arts, not the dark arts. There is much work to be done. "In today's world there are more health care professionals involved in the design and structuring of torture than there are involved in providing care for survivors," said Douglas Johnson, executive director of the Center for Victims of Torture, in Minneapolis, on *Democracy Now!*[26]

The grassroots revolt among psychologists is spreading, often in spontaneous acts of conscience. Just days after the APA convention in 2007, psychologist Mary Pipher heard Steven Reisner and Stephen Soldz discuss the interrogation controversy on *Democracy Now!* Pipher is the author of the best-selling book *Reviving Ophelia* and *In the Middle of Everywhere,* a book about refugees and torture survivors. She promptly decided on her own to return the President's Citation that she had received from the APA. She wrote, "I do not want an award from an organization that sanctions its members' participation in the enhanced interrogations at CIA 'black sites' and at Guantánamo."

In late 2007, six college psychology departments—Earlham, Guilford, California State University at Long Beach, University of Rhode Island, York College of the City

University of New York, and Smith College—went on record saying that it was a violation of professional ethics for psychologists to participate in interrogations in any prison outside the United States where there is a lack of due process. Other psychology departments are considering similar resolutions. And a number of APA members are withholding dues (withholdapadues.com) in protest against the organization's stance.

We sat with Reisner at the APA convention shortly after the moratorium on interrogations, for which he'd crusaded for two years, was defeated. His eyes welled and his voice cracked as he reflected on the outcome. "I was a psychologist, and I wanted to close the door [to torture]. I thought I could." He has vowed to press on.

Jean Maria Arrigo reflected on what made her stand up. "I didn't want to be that person who couldn't make a small move because it would hurt a little bit. That's what it takes. You have to take a small move that's going to hurt."

III. *Students Standing* **UP**

Standing Up to the Madness in 1976: The Soweto Uprising

On June 16, 1976, schoolchildren in Soweto, the sprawling black township outside Johannesburg, South Africa, revolted. They poured into the streets to protest a new apartheid law requiring that they be taught in Afrikaans, "the language of the oppressor," as Archbishop Desmond Tutu once called the mother tongue of white Afrikaners. The students' act of defiance that day would change the course of their nation's history.

"The most potent weapon in the hands of the oppressor is the mind of the oppressed," said Steve Biko, leader of South Africa's Black Consciousness Movement and an inspiration to student activists. A cornerstone of oppression in South Africa was "Bantu education," the name given to the separate and inferior schooling that South Africa's black majority was forced to endure under the system of official discrimination known as apartheid. Biko charged that the objective of Bantu education was "to prepare the black man for the subservient role in this country."

Throughout South Africa in 1976, parents and teachers objected to the imposition of Afrikaans in the schools. These objections fell on deaf ears. So students decided to wage a nonviolent protest to register their opposition to the apartheid government policies. On June

13, 1976, Tsietsi Mashinini, a 19-year-old Soweto student leader, called a meeting of students to plan a walkout and march several days later.

On the morning of June 16, 1976, thousands of black students streamed out of their schools in a peaceful march to Orlando Stadium, where they intended to hold a rally. But police blocked the way, then shot tear gas and finally opened fire on the unarmed children. More than five hundred students were killed that day.

The Soweto Uprising might have received little attention were it not for an iconic photo of a dying 12-year-old, Hector Pieterson, being carried by grief-stricken Mbuyisa Makhuba, accompanied by Hector's sister, Antoinette. The image, taken by photographer Sam Nzima for a black newspaper, was splashed across front pages around the world the next day. The combination of student activism and grassroots media attention emboldened anti-apartheid activists both inside and outside South Africa.

The student revolt in Soweto was a turning point in South Africa's liberation struggle. In the months following the protest, international condemnation rained down on South Africa. The United Nations tightened sanctions against the racist regime. But it was students around the world who made the global campaign against apartheid into a local issue in their communities.

Students throughout the United States and Europe pressured universities and governments to divest from stocks in companies that were profiting from apartheid. By spring 1977, almost three hundred students protesting apartheid were arrested at Stanford University, and Hampshire College in Massachusetts became the first university to respond to student demands by selling $215,000 in stock. By 1979, universities were divesting more than $25 million per year. By 1991, 28 states, 24 counties, and 92 cities had passed divestment legislation.

The Soweto Uprising galvanized a new generation of activists inside South Africa. It was these leaders, backed by liberation movements and solidarity groups, that ultimately led to Nelson Mandela's release from prison in 1990 and his election as South Africa's first democratic president in 1994.

Where students led, the world followed. The downfall of apartheid was hastened by the courage and sacrifice of young people in South Africa. Today, that struggle is memorialized in the Hector Pieterson Museum in Soweto, and June 16 is celebrated annually in South Africa as Youth Day.

As South African students chanted in 1976, "Amandla ngawethu!"—power to the people! Through their actions, they showed the world the true meaning of their rallying cry.

CHAPTER 6

Voices in Conflict

Jimmy Presson was freaking out. The 16-year-old junior from Wilton High School in Connecticut was pacing in a corner, going over his lines for the school play. He had a powerful monologue to deliver, and he wanted to get it right. He was playing the part of an Iraq War veteran, Navy Hospital Corpsman Charlie Anderson. The vet was describing his struggles with post-traumatic stress disorder (PTSD).

Finally, the house lights dimmed. Jimmy stepped forward, his feet spread in a defiant stance, his demeanor a bit bewildered, like the seaman whose life he was channeling:

> *My symptoms didn't show up right away. Then everything just caught up to me and hit me all at once. . . . You get home, you relax, and then it just comes rushing up. I have nightmares. I can't sleep.*[1]

There was a dramatic pause, and Jimmy exhaled. As he looked out, he didn't see the faces of friends and families in the Wilton High School auditorium, the venue for other school plays in which he had acted. Instead, he was peering from the stage of the Culture Project, a theater in SoHo. The audience was New York City theater buffs.

When Jimmy Presson signed up for Theater Arts II taught by teacher Bonnie Dickinson in the spring of 2007, he and the other students couldn't have imagined in their wildest dreams that they would end up performing in a New York City theater. Professional actors only hope of getting a break like this. Jimmy and the rest of the cast were just high school students who had spent the spring preparing to perform for their friends and families. Suddenly, their student play, *Voices in Conflict,* was banned from Wilton High School.

Was there graphic sex? Homosexuality? Violence?

No—but the theater arts students had done plays that dealt with all those hot-button issues in previous years without incident or objection from the school administration. *Voices in Conflict* dealt with a topic that was much too hot to discuss in this suburban Connecticut school.

The subject was war.

When Wilton High School tried to silence the student actors in the spring of 2007, the students of Wilton and their teacher mounted a national stage. Their courageous stand shed light on the pervasive silencing of critical voices, especially when those voices are veterans telling the story of living and dying in a war they have been sent to fight in our name.

We find Bonnie Dickinson sitting at an outside table at a café on a warm summer afternoon in the picturesque village of Wilton. This suburban community of eighteen thousand lies less than an hour from New York City, but its sense of cloistered affluence makes it seem a world away. A group of students and parents have joined us to talk about the experience of being banned, shunned, and then hailed and celebrated. It has been two months since their last curtain call, but the outrage and exhilaration of their experience comes bubbling back with each retelling.

Dickinson has been the drama teacher at Wilton High School since 1993. A 53-year-old mother of two, she is dressed in jeans and a stylish blue blouse, her face framed by a mane of blond hair. Her students casually alternate between "Bonnie" and "Mrs. Dickinson" when addressing her. She is hip enough to connect with them, but also commands their respect.

Dickinson graduated from New York University in 1976 and struggled to survive as an actress doing off-off-Broadway shows; she later cofounded an experimental multiracial Shakespeare company in Los Angeles. A popular teacher, her classes at Wilton High School, which is home to 1,250 students, typically have waiting lists. She is well known in the school and community as the director of the fall play and the drama club. Dickinson is not involved in Wilton High School's extravagant spring musicals—*West Side Story* and *Grease* were some of the recent productions—which are performed in a $10 million state-of-the-art theater. She prefers the "intimate, shabby Little Theater" for her dramatic performances.

Dickinson's real passion is educational theater, which she offers to students in several theater arts classes. She often uses drama to tackle difficult and sensitive issues within the school community. Several years ago, when Wilton High School was the scene of gay bashing incidents and some lockers had been defaced with racial epithets, Dickinson and her students chose to perform *The Laramie Project*. The play, about the murder of Matthew Shepard, a young gay man in Wyoming, was "a big success. Only one parent out of a thousand said we don't want our kid to do it," she recalls. The administration had been concerned about the subject matter, but agreed to allow the play to be performed for juniors and seniors.

In the fall of 2006, Dickinson was looking for a new way to engage her students. As she often did, the drama teacher stopped by the school library to see what new books looked interesting. The English Department chairwoman, Sandy Soson, was also prowling the stacks looking for material. By chance, the two teachers stumbled upon the same book, *In Conflict: Iraq War Veterans Speak Out on Duty, Loss and the Fight to Stay Alive,* by Yvonne Latty. The book is a collection of first-person accounts from soldiers about their experiences fighting in Iraq and Afghanistan.

"Teachers are always looking for voices of kids their age," Dickinson tells us. "I saw the book as a collection of great monologues. There's nothing like a first-person anecdote to connect with the audience. This was a natural piece of theater." Dickinson planned to offer the soldiers' monologues to her theater arts students and see whether it captured their interest.

A personal play about war was especially timely. Wilton High School had been shaken that fall by the news that Nicholas Madaras, a 2005 Wilton graduate who had joined the army, had been killed in Iraq by a roadside bomb. It gave further impetus to Dickinson's interest in offering the students a play that dealt with the war. When she approached principal Timothy Canty in November 2006 with *In Conflict,* she recalls that he said that the idea of a play based on the book "sounds great."

"You might even honor Nick in it," Canty told her. Dickinson agreed. It was a routine approval.

When Theater Arts II met in January 2007, Dickinson was contacted by a parent, Barbara Alessi, who had a son serving in the military in Iraq and whose daughter was initially signed up for Dickinson's class. Alessi complained to both Dickinson and Canty that the play was "anti-war." It hadn't occurred to Dickinson that the soldiers' real-life experience of combat could be construed as pro- or anti-war.

On March 9, Canty called Dickinson. "I don't wanna hear from this parent anymore," Dickinson recalls Canty telling her. "Shut this play down *now.*" (Canty, along with the members of the Wilton school board and Superintendent Gary Richards, declined our requests for comment.)

Dickinson pleaded for more time to change the script to make it more "balanced." She spent a frantic weekend working with teacher Sandy Soson to add more explicitly pro-war voices to counter any perception of bias. But when she presented the revised script to Canty, he was unconvinced.

The administration's rationale for shutting down the play began shifting. Dickinson says Canty told her, "I'm very concerned about the sister of the soldier who died. She should not have this going on in school." Then he complained that a revised script was too violent. Later, he claimed that the script was plagiarized, since it drew heavily on other books and a documentary film, *The Ground Truth,* allegedly without attribution.

"We tried to make sense of it, but there was no making

sense," Dickinson tells us, waving her hand in exasperation.

Canty informed Dickinson that the play could not go on. It was a few weeks before the performance. Dickinson insisted that he explain to the students in person why he was taking this action. On March 13, 2007, Canty met the students in the school theater, where they had been working on the play for two months.

"You can't do this play," he told them flatly. He said it was too controversial, too complicated. And just to be sure they understood, Dickinson recounts that he added, "You can't do this anywhere. You can work on it. But you can never perform it."

Students protested. Senior Erin Clancy, her voice trembling, said, "I'm 18—old enough to fight in the war, and old enough to vote for leaders who send people to war. So why can't I perform in a play about it?"

One student began swearing at the principal. Dickinson admonished the student and insisted that Canty be treated with respect.

Canty said his decision was final. He had made up his mind and would not debate the matter any further. "This ship has sailed," he told them.

Jimmy Presson was disgusted. Canty may have mollified one student and parent, but "he was hanging us out to dry."

> We all become casualties of war. Who we are when we leave is not who we are when and if we're lucky to physically return. Because psychologically, you, you, you're completely changed by it.
>
> —Corp. Sean Huze, from *The Ground Truth*, read by senior Seth Kopronski, *Voices in Conflict*[2]

Backlash

Students debated how to respond. One suggested letters to the editor. Another wanted to picket. Then an irate parent of one of the theater arts students contacted a reporter at the *New York Times.* On March 24, 2007, the *Times* ran a story describing how Wilton High School was shutting down a play about the Iraq War.

"Our school is all about censorship," Jimmy Presson was quoted in the article as saying. "People don't talk about the things that matter."[3]

Principal Tim Canty countered, "It would be easy to look at this case on first glance and decide this is a question of censorship or academic freedom. In some minds, I can see how they would react this way. But quite frankly, it's a false argument," he told the *Times.*

The response was swift and stunning. Invitations began to arrive for the students to perform in major theaters in New York City, including the prestigious Public Theater. Theater professionals of the Dramatists Guild of America, among whom were playwrights Edward Albee and Stephen Sondheim, sent letters of protest to Superintendent Gary Richards. The National Coalition Against Censorship called for the show to go on. Music Theatre International, an agency that licenses many high school productions, awarded the students its first ever "Courage in Theatre" award.

Voices in Conflict was in the spotlight after all.

Then the recriminations began. "Theater fag," "traitor" were just some of the names posted on a Facebook Web page about the students. The sixteen members of the cast found themselves shoved in the school hallways and shunned in the cafeteria. "It was horrible," says Presson of the aftermath. Through it all, the students stayed focused on their goal: bringing their play to the widest possible audience.

Meanwhile, the Wilton High School administration was digging in against the students. Superintendent Gary Richards issued a letter that stated: "The student performers directly acting the part of the soldiers . . . turns powerful material into a dramatic format that borders on being sensational and inappropriate. We would like to work with the students to complete a script that fully addresses our concerns."

Richards continued, "We believe that this play can be upsetting to our student, parent, and community audience. . . . As a school, we have a responsibility to ensure that the Iraq war, the lives lost, and the sacrifices made by soldiers and their families are presented in the appropriate context with appropriate support and guidance. . . . In its present form, the play does not meet those standards."

The students responded the way they knew best: They promptly added Richards's letter to the script. The cold, condescending bureaucratese would be in stark relief opposite the play's passionate eyewitness testimonials.

Jimmy Presson, dressed in a Jimi Hendrix T-shirt with a baseball cap pulled over his eyes, tells us that the battle was often isolating. "It felt like we were being kind of separated, like Wilton High School feels this way, and those students feel that way. That hurt a lot. . . . I don't hate my high school. I'm not trying to bring down the administration.

"We're not attacking *anyone* here," he says, his voice rising in anger. "The play wasn't meant to make people feel bad, or make people feel war was bad. It wasn't Democrats versus Republicans. None of this was a factor when we did the play."

Bonnie Dickinson became the subject of attacks. Barbara Alessi wrote an op-ed piece for the *Wilton Bulletin* declaring, "Though the play was to be an indictment of the troops, Ms. Dickinson was misrepresenting intent from the very beginning. . . . This was never about the ideal of freedom of speech. It was about the manipulative use and abuse of that principle by a vindictive teacher who used the hot button issue to attract the attention of the *New York Times*."

Alessi concluded with a veiled threat: "Does Ms. Dickinson believe that the media firestorm would inoculate her from all negative repercussions once the uproar died down and her actions were exposed? If she does, I believe she is wrong."[4] Alessi then filed a lengthy administrative complaint against Dickinson in late April.

Meanwhile, the national media shone a light on political censorship in Wilton. The students appeared on CNN and ABC's *Good Morning America,* and were featured in articles from the *Los Angeles Times* to the *Christian Science Monitor*. In response, the administration hedged, but didn't relent. In April, Principal Canty announced that it might be possible to have the play performed in school in the fall—after half the cast graduated.

Dickinson and the student actors had already shifted their energies into preparing for performances at the Public Theater, the Culture Project, and the Vineyard Theater in New York, and at the Fairfield Theater in Connecticut. In early June, an assistant superintendent again asked to see the script, which now included the superintendent's letter. "*This* is the version you want to do for school?" the administrator asked Dickinson.

"Now it is," Dickinson shot back.

Dickinson was emboldened, but nervous. "I was really scared for my job," she tells us as we have coffee with her and the students in Wilton. Cars honk nearby en route to a Wilton High School football game. A cancer survivor and mother, Dickinson could not afford to be fired. Noted First Amendment lawyer Martin Garbus volunteered to defend her and assured her that she would not lose her job.

The school's clumsy attempt to salvage its image ended up ensuring that Wilton's name became synonymous with censorship. "Had the school not done any of this stuff," said Garbus of the play, "it would have just gone through uneventfully."

The experiences I have had in the last two years have brought me down, but hopefully I'll get stronger. I just got to get there.

—Army Reserves Sgt. Lisa Haynes, from *In Conflict,* by Yvonne Latty, read by senior Erin Clancy, *Voices in Conflict*

Censorship Society

"Striving for Excellence" declares the slogan over the front door of Wilton High School. Indeed, Wilton is one of Connecticut's top public schools. But when it comes to discussing the war in Iraq, the school's motto would more accurately be "Striving for Silence."

When Wilton High School administrators banned *Voices in*

Conflict, they shut down the only place in school where the Iraq War was being vigorously discussed. Jimmy Presson, who was named after an uncle who was killed in the Vietnam War, tells us that his U.S. history class had a weekly assignment to bring in a current event news item, with one caveat: "We are not allowed to talk about the war while discussing current events." Other students said they could discuss the war in a Middle Eastern Studies class, but it was not being taught that spring. So it fell to Theater Arts II to be the only class in school where students were discussing the war in any depth.

Actually, there is one other place where students talk about war. "We also get to speak about it with the military recruiters who are always at school," says Presson wryly.

Wilton High School has a history of muzzling free speech. Students were upset in 2007 because the administration required that yearbook quotations come from well-known sources, out of fear they might contain coded messages. When the school's Gay Straight Alliance hung posters a few years ago, the administration ordered that all student posters be approved in advance, due to public safety concerns. Wilton administrators attempted to ban bandanas, insisting they could be associated with gangs. Officials were forced to back down when hundreds of bandana-wearing students showed up at school.[5]

Wilton High School is not alone in attempting to banish controversy from the mouths of its babes. In whitewashing dissent, it has taken a page from the script followed by President George W. Bush.

At the start of the Iraq War, Bush issued an executive order banning photos of soldiers' caskets returning from Iraq and Afghanistan, neatly decoupling the disastrous war from its body count. Following Hurricane Katrina, the Bush administration's decisive intervention was to ban images of dead bodies floating down the boulevards of New Orleans. And President Bush's advance team has banished protesters from appearing anyplace where cameras might capture them. It is all part of an elaborate effort to create a Potemkin presidency, where reality is defined and managed by those in power.

Beat poet Allen Ginsberg explained the rationale best: "Whoever controls the media, the images, controls the culture."

In this environment of manipulated imagery and suppression of free speech, it is no surprise that censorship in schools is on the rise:

- At John Jay High School in Cross River, New York (about fifteen miles from Wilton), three high school girls were suspended in March 2007 for reading an excerpt of Eve Ensler's play, *The Vagina Monologues,* during an open mic night at school. Their crime: uttering the word "vagina" after being warned not to. Parents decried the "blatant attempt at censorship," and the suspension was overturned.
- In March 2006, high school geography teacher Jay Bennish was suspended from Overland High School in Aurora, Colorado, following a class in which he criticized President Bush. Bennish's talk was recorded by a student, who gave it to local radio stations. In response to Bennish's suspension, more than one hundred students walked out of class. Bennish was reinstated several days later.

- Deborah A. Mayer, a teacher at an Indiana elementary school, lost her job after discussing the Iraq War. The class was reading about the impending war in the newsmagazine *Time for Kids* in January 2003 when the students in her grade 3–6 multiage class asked if she had ever protested. Mayer replied that she had honked when passing a demonstration where someone held a sign saying "Honk for Peace." After a parent complained, the principal barred Ms. Mayer from discussing "peace" in her classroom and canceled the school's traditional "peace month." The school announced a few months later that Mayer would not be rehired.

For Wilton parent Hermon Telyan, whose daughter Taylor acted in *Voices in Conflict,* being censored struck a familiar and chilling chord. Telyan, an Armenian who fled persecution in Turkey, is emotional as he tells us about his experience. "I lived fascism and repression. It is very familiar to me. I can smell fascism in a crowd.

"The first rule of fascism is censorship in the arts," he explains. Wilton administrators articulated it "in such a nice way I have to applaud. We have here a first-class fascist mentality. It came from Washington to Wilton."

While the debate over the banned play filled the pages of local newspapers—one parent said it was the most heavily covered local story he'd seen in his twenty-two years in Wilton—"the administration, the faculty, and the students became eerily silent on the matter," recalls Glen Clancy, whose daughter Erin was in the play. "The silence of the populace involved is one of the things I find most disturbing in the dynamics of censorship."

Ira Levin, author of *The Stepford Wives,* the best-selling novel and movie that depicts a town in which people are blindly conformist, wrote a letter to the *New York Times* immediately after the story about the play banning. Levin, who died in November 2007, drew the connection between fact and fiction:

> Wilton, Conn., where I lived in the 1960s, was the inspiration for Stepford, the fictional town I later wrote about in *The Stepford Wives.*
>
> I'm not surprised, therefore, to learn that Wilton High School has a Stepford principal, one who would keep his halls and classrooms squeaky-clean of any "inflammatory" material that might hurt some Wilton families.
>
> It's heartening, though, to know that not all the Wilton High students have been Stepfordized. The ones who created and rehearsed the banished play *Voices in Conflict* are obviously thoughtful young people with minds of their own.
>
> I salute them.[6]

Another letter to the *Times* helpfully suggested a play that would be perfectly suited to Wilton High School and its administration: a stage adaptation of George Orwell's *1984.*

> *I've spent hours taking in the world through a rifle scope, watching life unfold. Women hanging laundry on a rooftop. Men haggling over a hindquarter of lamb in the market. Children walking to school. I've watched this and hoped that someday I would see that my presence had made their lives better, a redemption of sorts. But I also peered through the scope waiting for some-*

*one to do something wrong, so I could shoot him. When you pick up
a weapon with the intent of killing, you step onto a very strange
and serious playing field. . . . You're all part of the terrible magic
show, both powerful and helpless. I miss Iraq. I miss the war.*
> —Brian Mockenhaupt, U.S. Army infantryman,
> read by junior Nick Lanza, *Voices in Conflict*[7]

*　　*　　*

We choose to hear the voices of those who serve.

The lone, determined voice echoes throughout the hall of
the Culture Project as the second New York City performance of *Voices in Conflict* opens. The theater is abuzz with ex-
citement, as the students jostle one another backstage to get
in position to take center stage.

Jimmy Presson, acting the part of Navy Seaman Charlie
Anderson, steps forward.

> *We take fire, we return fire. The military taught us how
> to pull the trigger but never once did they tell us what to do
> next.*
>
> *I heard it takes eleven or twelve years to adapt to being home.
> But right now, I don't even feel like I have a home. It's like I
> went away to war and someone secretly replaced my country. No
> one really understands me.*
>
> *The doctors say I have post-traumatic stress disorder.
> Disorder? I call it post-traumatic stress order. I'm worried about
> the guys who go through what we did and be normal.*[8]

Then it's Devon Fontaine's turn. The thin, dark-haired
high school student takes on the persona of Marine Sgt.

Robert Sarra. He tells a harrowing story of what happened one day when a woman in a burka approached him.

I pulled up my rifle, took two shots at her. I know I probably missed the first shot. The second shot, I'm pretty sure I hit her. And as soon as that second shot went off, the guys on the other vehicle opened up and they cut her down. She fell to the dirt, and as she fell, she had a, a white flag in her hand.

At that moment there, I lost it. I threw my weapon down on the deck of the vehicle and I was crying and I was like "Oh my god, what are we doing here? What's happening?"

I had a gunnery sergeant who had been in the first war. He said it happens. There's nothing you can do to bring her back. It happens. We got to keep going.[9]

Devon tells us back in Wilton, "Thinking about that woman coming toward my vehicle and shooting her once, twice—yeah it is very violent. But that's what war is.

"Every time I did that monologue, I saw that woman, I shot her. . . . It affected me every time—in a good way. It put me in the shoes of this soldier. I really felt like I was there."

Courtney Stack, a junior and the choreographer for the play, hadn't thought much about Iraq before the play. "You have these numbers thrown at you about how many died today, yesterday—after being exposed to that, you sort of become numb to it. . . . Seeing other kids assuming the roles of these different people, it changes it from just a number to realizing these are people who are not that different from who we are. That makes such an astonishing impression." Courtney reflected on the impact that each soldier's death has had on their families and communities. "I think of how it would feel if a couple hundred students didn't show up for school one day. That's the real effect of this war."

At the end of the play, students step forward, one by one, to introduce themselves—in the words of others.

> *And so we serve those who serve by telling their stories.*
> *Who are we?*
> *Rebels without a cause.*
> *Fucking Goths.*
> *Femme-Nazi teacher.*
> *Stupid.*
> *Worthless.*
> *Theater fags.*
> *Liberal pig parents.*
> *Disrespectful.*
> *Immature.*
> *Unpatriotic.*
> *Unabashedly biased.* [10]

Then one by one, the actors challenge those who tried to silence them:

> *Why is talking about the war "sensational and*
>   *inappropriate"?*
> *Since when has war not been graphic and violent?*
> *If they consider the words of the soldiers biased, why do they*
>   *allow an army recruiter into the school cafeteria?*

Why has the school been silent on these issues?
Why did it take a New York Times *article to start*
      discussion?[11]

As the curtain falls on the last monologue, the audience rises in a long standing ovation. Some people have tears in their eyes. Culture Project artistic director Allan Buchman speaks. "I couldn't be more proud of having this work on our stage. It should travel around the country. Why it is not shown [in Wilton] is beyond my comprehension. What we saw tonight," he said, "is the reason to have a theater."

Actor Stanley Tucci, who starred in *The Devil Wears Prada,* had visited Wilton to interview the students after the play was banned. He says, "I suddenly felt there was some hope that theater was not just indulgent but can actually do some good, and some damage, in a good way." He then addressed the students and their teacher. "You've made the people of Connecticut very proud."

Devon talks to us after the performance about what he gained. "I learned that you've gotta fight for what you believe in."

Natalie Kropf, an ebullient senior, says, "I don't think I've ever learned so much from anything I've done. Some soldiers came two nights ago. They came backstage and said, 'You guys nailed it two hundred percent.' I just felt so proud."

The parents agree. Moira Rizzo, whose daughter Allie was in the play, tells us, "I would say it was the most meaningful, inspiring thing that has happened to us as her parents yet. I wouldn't trade this personal growth experience for my kid for anything in the world. It's a shame because this was an opportunity for everyone to look fantastic. Bonnie and the kids came out shining, and the school system came out looking like a bunch of fools."

Glen Clancy, father of actress Erin, observed that in defying their banning order, the students learned more than they'd ever imagined. "They learned that those in authority to whom they have given unquestioned respect can suddenly turn devious and duplicitous when it's time to cover their own butts. They learned bravery by watching their now beloved teacher endure job-threatening actions from the school and stand tall in their defense because what they were doing was the right thing to do. They were presented with Music Theatre International's 'Courage in Theatre' award, but every one of them will tell you the real courage was displayed by Bonnie Dickinson. Now, *that* is a role model."

Dickinson's ordeal continued even after the performances finished. In August 2007, the school administration released the results of the investigation that it did in response to Barbara Alessi's complaint. The school found that almost all of the charges leveled by Alessi were unsubstantiated. But the school insisted that Dickinson did not cite her sources properly. In fact, the students identified the source for each of their monologues during the performances, but Wilton officials would not have known: Not a single Wilton administrator attended any of the nine performances that were staged in New York City and Connecticut theaters in June and July 2007.

In November 2007, Dickinson and her former Theater Arts II students traveled to New York City again. This time they came to receive an award from the National Coalition Against Censorship, which recognized them for "their courage in writing and performing *Voices in Conflict*."

Bonnie Dickinson continues to feel harassed by school officials, but vindicated by her students. We ask her why she fought. She is in a hurry—she has to conduct a rehearsal for the fall play, a hip-hop version of Shakespeare's *Twelfth Night*—but she pauses to answer.

"For the kids. I could not let them down. . . . I realized this is where my whole life was going. . . . I love these kids. I love doing theater. And that's it. I could care less what the administration says about me."

She pauses a moment and just shakes her head as she ponders all that has happened. "This censorship was so blatant. Fifty-five minutes from New York City, in 2007," she sputters in exasperation. "Didn't they ever learn anything? Here we are fighting for democracy in Iraq—that's the irony of it all."

For one of their last performances at the Public Theater in New York, the parents and students decided to buy a plane ticket for Charlie Anderson to fly in. He was the navy seaman with PTSD whose words were brought to life by Jimmy Presson. As the show ended, Anderson walked up to Jimmy and embraced him in a giant bear hug. He then pinned his medic badge on Jimmy.

"The navy's core values are honor, courage, and commitment," Anderson told the student actors, "and I can say beyond any doubt that you all exemplified all of them."

STUDENT: *Who are we?*

CAST: *Just some kids from Connecticut.*

We are not the future of America. We are *America. One love.*

CHAPTER 7

Justice in Jena

Robert Bailey, Jr., was excited to start the new school year at Jena High School. He and his friends on the Jena Giants football team, including Mychal Bell, Bryant Purvis, Carwin Jones, and Jesse Beard, had been working hard in preseason practices to get ready for upcoming games. Attention was focused on Bell to carry the team to victory. College scouts had been coming from afar to watch the ferociously talented star running back from this town of three thousand people in rural Louisiana. The coach thought Bell had what it took to play in the NFL—just like Bryant Purvis's uncle, Jason Hatcher, a former star for the Jena Giants who is now on the Dallas Cowboys.

On August 30, 2006, the boys gathered for a school assembly. After school officials gave an obligatory review of school rules, the freshman Justin Purvis, who is African-American, asked if he and his friends could sit under the White Tree. This was the broad leafy tree that spread over the open-air courtyard of Jena High School. It was the unofficial hangout spot for white students.

A lot of things in Jena are like that: Things that have been a certain way in the past just continue that way. Black people, who comprise about one-fifth of the community, live in a black neighborhood that receives no trash pickup. White neighborhoods, including an area everyone calls Snob Hill, are fully serviced by the town.

But the young people see Jena with fresh eyes. They question the status quo. That's where change—and trouble—begins. Justin Purvis's simple question that day was to trigger a racist miscarriage of justice that threatened to ruin the lives of six young black men. It has evolved into an affirmation of the redemptive power of youth, family, activism, and courage. The fierce resistance of a few black families in Jena, Louisiana, has unalterably changed the national dialogue about race and justice.

"You can sit anywhere you like," replied an administrator. So Justin, his cousin Bryant Purvis, and several other African-American students ventured into forbidden terrain. They relaxed under the White Tree that afternoon. It provided cool relief from the relentless southern sun. But it touched a raw nerve in those who saw it as a challenge to white privilege.

The following morning, students arrived at school to find several nooses hanging from the branches of the tree. Robert Bailey was only 17. But as an African-American, he knew immediately and viscerally what those nooses meant. "The first thing came to mind was the KKK," he told us one evening in his mother's trailer. His black jacket bore a large gold varsity letter "J," which he had earned playing football and basketball at Jena High. "I used to always think the KKK chased black people on horses, and they catch you with a rope."

The KKK is no stranger to Jena. Former assistant school

superintendent Cleveland Riser, who is African-American, told us that years back he had confronted hooded Klansmen driving around Goodpine, a black neighborhood. Jena's white residents voted overwhelmingly for KKK leader David Duke when he ran unsuccessfully for Louisiana governor in 1991.[1]

Nooses are a deadly serious symbol, especially in the Deep South. From the 1880s to the 1960s, at least 4,700 men and women were lynched in the United States, many of them in the South. More than 70 percent of the victims were African-Americans.[2]

Tensions spiked at Jena High. Black students questioned white students to find out who hung the nooses. Fights broke out. School principal Scott Windham took the threat seriously. He identified the three white students who hung the nooses and recommended they be expelled. But an expulsion committee recommended a three-day suspension; they were backed by Superintendent Roy Breithaupt, who overruled Windham. "Adolescents play pranks," Breithaupt explained to the *Chicago Tribune*. "I don't think it was a threat against anybody."[3] Shortly after, Scott Windham was replaced as principal.

Black students protested the noose incident, again peacefully gathering under the White Tree. That caught the attention of local law enforcement. On September 6, 2006, LaSalle Parish district attorney Reed Walters showed up at school for an assembly, backed by armed local police. It was an intimidating show of force. The short, bespectacled white D.A. with close-cropped hair and a piercing gaze warned the students to stop making a fuss about the "innocent prank."

"I can be your best friend or your worst enemy," he warned them. Then he held up his pen in the air for effect and declared, "I can make your life go away with the stroke of a pen." The black students say he was staring directly at them as he spoke.[4] Three months later, Walters would prove what he meant.

But first, there was sports. The high school football team is the main attraction for the community. The sign greeting visitors into town says as much: "Jena—Home of the Jena Giants." On a visit to Jena High School, home to about five hundred students, we saw the outsized importance of the school teams. The no-frills academic campus—the aging tan brick buildings connected by breezeways have the feel of a sleepy working-class suburban school—sit in the shadow of the light towers that soar over the school football stadium. The well-worn gym lobby gleams with the gold and silver trophies of past sports triumphs. The school's basketball team is a periodic contender for the state championships.

In the fall of 2006, Mychal Bell was the undisputed star of the Jena Giants. The only Jena player to make the All-State football team, the tall, solidly built 16-year-old African-American boy had a rare combination of talents: He had quick reflexes, was a fast runner, and could play offense as well as he played defense. Jena's veteran football coach figured Bell was a shoo-in to be recruited onto a Division 1 college team, and scouts from Louisiana State University, Mississippi State, and others had already expressed interest.

When the 2006 football season ended, trouble in Jena began in earnest. Incidents between white and black students had simmered all fall. Then, on the night of November 30, 2006, a suspicious fire destroyed the main academic building of Jena High School. Investigators determined that the fire had resulted from arson. Whites and blacks accused each other of involvement in the crime, which many local people believe was related to the noose incident.

On Friday night, December 1, Robert Bailey was beaten by a group of white students when he showed up at a private party. He charges that he was hit over the head with a beer bottle. When the police arrived, he says they warned him, "Get back to your side of town."

The next night, Bailey, Theo Shaw, and a friend were at the Gotta' Go convenience store, a local hangout. They encountered one of the white men who'd beaten Bailey. There was a confrontation, and the white man ran to his truck and returned with a shotgun. Bailey, a strapping athlete, quickly wrestled the shotgun away from him. The boys returned home, and Bailey says he reported the incident and the weapon to the police. Three Jena policemen subsequently showed up at his mother's trailer and began interrogating him, ignoring his mother's demands for information. The police confiscated the shotgun, which was equipped with a pistol grip and laser scope. Then they charged Bailey with robbery and conspiracy—for stealing the weapon.

"The police were more concerned about the shotgun than they were about the safety of my kid," said Robert's incredulous mother, Caseptla Bailey, as we spoke with her on a sultry summer evening at her home. The young white man who attacked Bailey at the party and later menaced him with a shotgun was later charged with simple battery and given probation.

After a long weekend of white-on-black attacks, which followed the arson and a long fall of racist taunts against black students, tensions were at the breaking point at school on Monday, December 4, 2006. At lunch in the cafeteria, a white student, Justin Barker, 17, allegedly taunted Robert Bailey for the beating he'd received at the party a few days earlier; some witnesses say he called Bailey a nigger. A fight then broke out with a group of black students. Barker was knocked to the ground, lost consciousness, and was punched and kicked by several students. Barker was treated at a local hospital and released, and returned to school that evening to attend a ring ceremony.

The Jena High School student handbook states that the penalty for fighting in school is a three-day suspension. But the incident was not treated as a schoolyard brawl. Suddenly, D.A. Reed Walters reappeared. He would handle this as a criminal matter. Six black students—Robert Bailey, Jr., 17; Carwin Jones, 18; Bryant Purvis, 17; Mychal Bell, 16; Theo Shaw, 17; and Jesse Beard, 15—were arrested for beating Barker. Walters charged the six with attempted second-degree murder and conspiracy to commit murder. The charges carried a possible sentence of twenty to one hundred years in prison for each boy. Bail ranged from $70,000 to $138,000. The six were all expelled from school.

The district attorney had made good on his threat to destroy their lives.

Few of the boys' families could afford the astronomical bail, and none could afford private attorneys. Mychal Bell languished in jail for eight months before his trial in July 2007. Shortly before trial, Bell was offered a plea bargain by Walters. Mychal's father, Marcus, would have none of it. "In LaSalle Parish, whenever a black man is offered a plea bargain, he is innocent. That's a dead giveaway here in the South," he told *Democracy Now!* in July 2007. Mychal Bell refused the plea bargain. The district attorney was reportedly furious.

D.A. Walters apparently did not have enough evidence to

make an attempted murder rap stick; he reduced the charges to second-degree assault and conspiracy—still a felony. The subsequent trial in July 2007 was a travesty of justice. One of the prosecution witnesses was a student involved in hanging the nooses in the tree. The felony assault charge stipulates that a deadly weapon has to have been used in the crime. So the district attorney conjured the weapon: Bell's sneakers. When it came time for Bell's defense, his court-appointed attorney offered none. To the horror of Bell's family, the lawyer called no witnesses. The all-white jury found Bell guilty on all counts. At the age of 17, the one-time football star saw his promising future extinguished.

"We Have to Fight for What's Right"

Then something happened in Jena. The boys' parents vowed to fight. A local minister offered his church for meetings. Caseptla Bailey, mother of Robert Bailey, began writing letters to the U.S. Department of Justice, Louisiana officials—anyone who would listen. "I never been politically active," she told us at her home one evening. It was busy at her small trailer, as friends and relatives were crowded into the adjoining living room. She continued, "We as black people have just gotten to a point where we don't need to take this anymore. We have to fight for what's right." The parents formed the Jena Six Defense Committee. After Jena Six family members mentioned the address of the defense committee on *Democracy Now!* in July 2007, they said $100,000 in donations poured in to help bail out their children and hire lawyers.

Activists also took interest in the case. Allan Bean, from

Friends of Justice, a civil rights organization based in Tulia, Texas—a town that saw 15 percent of its black population arrested in a bogus drug sting in 1999—took notice of the apartheid justice being meted out in Jena. He began to champion the case of the Jena Six. Jordan Flaherty, a New Orleans community activist and journalist, broke the story about the case in early May 2007 in *Left Turn,* a national independent magazine. Soon after, the mainstream media began to take an interest. A *Chicago Tribune* reporter, Howard Witt, traveled to Jena in May 2007 and wrote a powerful series of articles about the boys' cases; a BBC story soon followed. Big Noise Films, *Democracy Now!*, and African-American bloggers and radio hosts took up the case. The ACLU, NAACP, and Southern Poverty Law Center got involved. Shortly after Mychal Bell's conviction in July 2007, the sleepy town was host to a rally of three hundred people demanding justice for the Jena Six.

The families and community of the Jena Six refused to be silenced.

White residents criticized the meddling of "outsiders." Caseptla Bailey countered, "I *love* outsiders. If it weren't for outsiders, our kids woulda been locked down and still be in prison."

By September 2007, the Jena Six case had snowballed into an international story about racism and injustice. CNN was running daily updates. The attention had an impact. Two weeks before Mychal Bell was to be sentenced, a local judge threw out Bell's conspiracy charge. His new lawyers made an emergency appeal of his assault conviction. A week before his sentencing, Louisiana's Third Circuit Court of Appeals threw out his assault conviction, saying it should have been filed in juvenile court, if at all.

Suddenly, the curtains were pulled back and a bright light shone in on the unequal system of justice that blacks routinely face in the Deep South and elsewhere.

But it takes more than the glare of publicity to beat back Jim Crow. It takes a movement. That arrived in Jena on September 20, 2007.

The buses began trundling down the sleepy streets of Jena before dawn. First it was hundreds of protesters, coming from as far away as Los Angeles, Chicago, North Carolina, and New York. Soon it was tens of thousands spilling out onto Jena's main street, where shops had closed for the day. By day's end, tens of thousands of people streamed into the small Louisiana town—likely the largest demonstration in rural Louisiana in modern times—to drive home a clear message. As one protester in Jena told filmmaker Rick Rowley on *Democracy Now!*, "Martin Luther King said that all ignorance should be tied together. And so justice in Jena, for us, is justice anywhere in the country."[5]

Civil rights leaders, including Rev. Jesse Jackson, Martin Luther King III, and Rev. Al Sharpton were there. So were rap stars Mos Def, Bun B, and Ice Cube. But there was no single leader of the march, so many mini-rallies occurred throughout the day of protest. The leaders were the families of the Jena Six, whose perseverance and courage had sparked a grassroots uprising. The rally was an expression of mass national revulsion against racism. It was an unimaginable show of force on behalf of the poor black residents who had been fighting what seemed like an impossible, quixotic battle against hundreds of years of unequal justice.

"This is the beginning of the twenty-first century's civil rights movement," Reverend Sharpton told the throng. "In the twentieth century, we had to fight for where we sat on the bus. Now, we've gotta fight on how we sit in a courtroom. We've gone from plantations to penitentiaries, where they have tried to create a criminal justice system that particularly targets our young black men."

Reed Walters, who had enjoyed unchecked power to make and destroy the black lives within his domain, was suddenly on the defensive. He came out onto the courthouse steps surrounded by armed police and stood beside Justin Barker, the white teen who was beaten up in school. (In May 2007, Barker had been arrested and expelled from school for having a rifle loaded with thirteen bullets hidden behind the seat of his pickup truck at Jena High School. He claims he forgot the gun was there.) Walters declared, "This case is not and never has been about race. It is about finding justice for an innocent victim and holding people accountable for their actions."

One week after the march, just hours before a Louisiana appeals court was to hear arguments on why Mychal Bell was still being held in jail after it had ruled that he had been wrongly tried as an adult, Reed Walters held a press conference to announce that he would not appeal the court's decision and would re-try Bell as a juvenile. In a bizarre conclusion, Walters offered his view of the civil rights march that occurred a week earlier, which was notably peaceful and at which there were no arrests. "I firmly believe and am confident of the fact that had it not been for the direct intervention of the lord Jesus Christ last Thursday, a disaster would have happened," said the small-town prosecutor, whose case and reputation were being trashed on the national stage. "You can quote me on that."

A judge promptly lowered Bell's bond to $45,000, which was immediately posted by a Louisiana physician. Mychal Bell walked out of jail ten months after being locked up.

Reverend Sharpton concluded at the civil rights rally, "Martin Luther King, Jr., and others faced Jim Crow. We come to Jena to face James Crow, Jr., Esquire. He's a little more educated. A little more polished. But it's the same courthouse steps used to beat down our people. And just like our daddies beat Jim Crow, we will win the victory over James Crow, Jr."

A History of Oppression

Racism in Jena didn't begin with the incidents at Jena High School. "Jena is an area that's got a whole history of oppression of black folks," said Curtis Muhammad, a veteran civil rights activist, as we chatted with him on his porch in New Orleans. "Those areas go back to being slave catchers. This is Mississippi in 1930. This is ugly."

Memories of segregation are still fresh in the minds of Jena's older generation of African-American residents. For them, the current racial tensions flow directly out of Jena's past. Cleveland Riser, Jr., is a 74-year-old former assistant superintendent of schools in LaSalle Parish. The highest-ranking black educator in the area, Riser retired in 1985, a year after winning a racial discrimination lawsuit against the school district. He lives on a street named after him in the community of Goodpine, where much of the black population lives around Jena. His well-kept brick home is an anchor in the community, a symbol of middle-class achievement. A tall, dignified man, he peers through thick glasses and offers to show us inside. He explains that he was principal of the former Goodpine High School, once an all-black school, whose students were integrated into Jena High School in 1969.

Riser points proudly to the football trophies his Goodpine teams earned. He originally had to fight to have a black football team and to get equipment from the school district; it was only after threatening to send all his players to sign up to play for Jena High that funds were found for him to field a team. We speak to him outside on his porch.

Ever since school integration, Riser says, there has been the sense among blacks "that Jena High School does not belong to black kids, it belongs to the white kids. And as a result of that, many black kids, many black parents, are saying that we have no school anymore."

Riser says the Jena Six case resulted from local white political figures who took the view, " 'We want to let [blacks] know what their place is, and we have an opportunity now to do this. . . . We want to make sure that they remember that there are some bridges you don't cross in Jena.' "

As we talk on his porch, music beats from the open door of a small house across the street where a man is fixing his car. Other small wooden houses line the street, many of them long overdue for a fresh coat of paint.

Riser insists that Jena is not unique. Raising his finger, he asserts, "We're just a little small part of America that became visible."

Billy Wayne Fowler, 68, is a lifelong Jena resident and a member of the LaSalle Parish School Board. Unlike every other town official whom we tried to interview, "Bulldog" Fowler was eager to speak with us. We meet with him where he works, at a church warehouse for distributing supplies to needy people. Wearing his red Jena Giants baseball cap and bulging red T-shirt, he tells us that he is deeply pained by how Jena's image has been tarnished. Jena "is a typical Deep South town. If I could take you back fifty years ago, a lot of this that's been said today may be true. But if you compare us today to fifty years ago, we have come a long way. We're still not perfect, but we still are Deep South Southerners.

"I don't think you will find anybody here that mistreats black folks. . . . We had a football game here a week ago, blacks and whites mixing without incident. Only a small portion of the black community here claims that we are racial. A big majority of the black folks will tell you they don't think it is."

As for the nooses hanging from the tree, Fowler says, "It was in a joking manner. Bad taste. Bad taste. Shouldn't have happened. But that's what was happening.

"Now, I know what's probably going through your mind: Now, this is the Deep South, and black people don't know the significance of a noose? Well, let me tell you something. The young black folks in the Deep South probably don't understand that. The older ones do, and they resent it, and I don't blame them."

Was a hate crime committed in Jena? "Now, who do you think more fits a hate crime here than anybody?" asks Fowler. "The six . . . It wasn't a fight. It was a planned deal."

Following the expulsion of the Jena Six, the students appealed their punishment to the school board. Billy Fowler had just been elected to the board, and the Jena Six appeal was the new board's first order of business in January 2007. The school district had conducted an investigation, but the school board was told it was not allowed to review it. The school board's lawyer was none other than the prosecuting district attorney, Reed Walters.

Board member Fowler recalls the January meeting: "Our legal authority that night was Mr. Walters."

We ask, "And he told you you couldn't have access to the school proceedings or the investigation?"

Fowler replies: "That's right. [Walters said] it was a violation of something." So the board voted, without information. "All we could do was vote on what we were told," he tells us.

Fowler recalls that the board vote "was unanimous." Then he corrects himself. "No, no it wasn't. There was one board member who voted no, and that was Mr. Worthington." Melvin Worthington, the only African-American on the school board, voted against expelling the black students.

Asked if he felt that Walters had a conflict of interest that night, Fowler replies, "Well, I'm assuming that Mr. Walters knows the law."

The conflict of interest was breathtaking: One day Walters was questioning the boys as a school official about what happened, and the next day he was using that same information to prosecute them for attempted murder. Had the LaSalle Parish school board determined that the Jena Six were innocent, it would have undermined Walters's attempted murder case in court.

For the Jena Six, there was no escape. The district attorney was intent on shutting down every avenue of appeal and fast-tracking the teens into prison. The school board just did what Walters told them to do. "We didn't know a whole lot," Fowler recounts, "so we voted to uphold [the expulsion]."

A few hours later, we visit the trailer that is home to Robert Bailey, Jr., and Theo Shaw, two of the Jena Six. A group of young men is crowded around a TV watching the football season opener for Grambling State, a college where Theo and Robert say they hope to attend and play sports. Robert's mother, Caseptla, is in the kitchen, along with several of her friends and neighbors. As the game finishes, thoughts turn to other things: Robert and Theo are planning to go out for the evening. The kitchen suddenly resembles a dry cleaner, as the boys carefully lay out their clothes, set up an ironing board, and begin pressing their pants and shirts. While they iron, we talk to them about their experiences over the past few months.

We ask Theo what the nooses meant to him when he saw them hanging from the White Tree. "A threat: 'We gonna kill you. We don't want you around here.' That's how I looked at it."

Did he think it was funny? A prank? "It wasn't no prank. It was a threat," he repeats.

Robert adds that the white students "should have got the same thing we got. It should have been equal. We got expelled. They should have got slammed. There shouldn't have been no second chance. They gave them a second chance to come back to school, gave them a good chance to get an education."

Instead, Theo and Robert were arrested and charged with attempted murder in December 2006, and their bail was set at $130,000 and $138,000, respectively. It took Robert's family five months to post the bond, and Theo's family seven months. During that time, the two boys languished in jail. Robert's grandmother, mother, and aunt had to use their homes as collateral for his freedom. The boys talk about how they tried to help each other survive in the harsh prison conditions.

Theo, baby-faced and soft-spoken, tells us how guards

would Mace the prisoners, triggering his asthma. The first time was March 14, 2007. Theo gasped from his cell, "I have asthma—take me to the emergency room! I can't breathe!"

Robert, thinking his friend was going to die, screamed frantically at the guards from his cell, "He can't breathe! He can't breathe!" He knew that he risked getting Maced for speaking up.

"I'm kicking the wall and jumping in front of the camera," Robert recalls. "They weren't going to believe us at first."

Theo says he was Maced repeatedly while in jail, causing asthma attacks that landed him in the hospital and at doctors' offices multiple times.

Why did they Mace you? "Sometimes when [prisoners] make a lot of noise, they'll Mace. And sometimes they just Mace for no reason," he replies.

The boys are almost done ironing. Robert dons his Jena Giants jacket, which has hung unused in his closet for a long time. Theo comes out in neatly pressed pants and a T-shirt, and they head out into the warm night.

From Schoolhouse to Jailhouse

The experience of the Jena Six is a microcosm of a phenomenon that is sweeping schools around the country: Instead of being sent to the principal, youths around the United States—especially minority youths—are being sent to jail. This is occurring despite the fact that between 1992 and 2002, school violence actually dropped by half nationwide.[6]

Many school arrests are for nonviolent offenses: In Florida during the 2005–2006 school year, more than three-quarters of the 26,990 school-related referrals to the Florida Department of Juvenile Justice were for misdemeanor offenses such as disorderly conduct, trespassing, or assault and/or battery (usually a schoolyard fight).[7]

"Florida's zero-tolerance policy is being used to criminalize petty acts of childish misconduct," said Monique Dixon, a senior attorney for the Advancement Project, a justice advocacy group. "Behavior once handled by a principal or a parent is now being handled by prosecutors and the police."[8]

As part of "zero-tolerance" discipline policies, schools are increasingly expelling and suspending problem students—especially children of color—rather than helping them. The *Chicago Tribune* found that in twenty-one states, the percentage of black student suspensions are more than double the percentage of blacks in the student body. Nationwide, black students are suspended and expelled at nearly three times the rate of white students. Yet there is no evidence that black students misbehave any more than other students.[9]

Children of color also are more likely to be referred by their school to the juvenile justice system. If a child is disabled, the outcome is even more bleak: African-American students with disabilities are three times more likely to be suspended as white students, and more than four times as likely to end up in correctional facilities.[10]

A half century after federal troops escorted nine black students into all-white Central High School in Little Rock, Arkansas, the inequalities in America's schools still run deep, especially when it comes to discipline.

These days, if you are a black student who gets in trouble in school, the odds are good that you will end up with a police record. Consider these bleak statistics:

- Denver—The Denver Public Schools experienced a 71 percent rise in the number of students referred to law enforcement between 2000 and 2004. Most referrals were for nonviolent behavior such as bullying and use of obscenities. Black and Latino students are 70 percent more likely to be disciplined (suspended, expelled, or ticketed) than their white peers.

- Chicago—More than eight thousand students were arrested in the Chicago Public Schools in 2003, mostly for simple assaults or batteries that involved no serious injuries or weapons. Seventy-seven percent of the arrests were of black students, although they comprise just half of the student population.[11]

- Florida—There was a 14 percent increase in the number of out-of-school suspensions from 2000 to 2005, culminating in an astounding 441,694 out-of-school suspensions in 2004–2005. Black students received 46 percent of out-of-school suspensions and police referrals statewide, but comprised only 22.8 percent of the student population.[12]

- New Jersey—African-American students are nearly sixty times as likely to be expelled from school for serious disciplinary problems as white students in New Jersey schools.[13]

Zero tolerance makes zero sense for kids. Take the case of Shaquanda Cotton, a 14-year-old African-American girl from Paris, Texas, who was sentenced in 2006 to seven years in prison for shoving a teacher's aide. The aide, who was not hurt, was preventing Cotton from entering the building before the beginning of the school day. Cotton spent a year in prison, until weeks of protests over her sentence led to her release in March 2007. Supporters say Cotton, who had no prior criminal record, was unfairly punished because she is black, and because of her mother's previous involvement in a group that fought discrimination against black students. The judge in the case, Chuck Superville of Lamar County, has been accused of double standards after he sentenced a 14-year-old white girl to probation for setting fire to her parents' house.[14]

"Children are being criminalized, handcuffed, arrested, booked, and sent to court for minor misconduct in school," declares a study undertaken by the Advancement Project and the NAACP. "This growing trend of relying upon law enforcement and the courts for typical, minor adolescent misbehavior . . . has dire consequences for children and their families and puts aside any notion of forgiving and teaching children."[15]

In Jena, the schoolhouse and the jailhouse are intimately connected: Jena is home to a notorious state prison run by the scandal-plagued private company GEO, formerly Wackenhut. Jena serves as a company town for the jail. Following Hurricane Katrina, the former juvenile prison, which had been closed since 2000, was reopened to house prisoners displaced by flooding in New Orleans. Abuse followed quickly. "Guards used racial slurs, forced prisoners to get up on tables and 'hop like bunnies' and threatened to force them to perform sex acts on guards," reported the *New York Times*. Attorney Rachel Jones, who surveyed reports from more than forty Louisiana prisons following the hurricane, said, "I did not hear anything even closely approximating the extreme levels of abuse and sadism that I heard at Jena. The inmates I spoke to repeatedly expressed that they were 'terrified' and 'scared for their lives' inside Jena."[16]

In July 2007, the GEO Group announced it was launching a $45 million expansion of the Jena facility, which will be used as an immigration prison capable of holding 1,160 detainees. The prison will have a workforce of more than 400 people, 254 of whom will be hired locally. The facility is expected to be completed in 2008. At the ground-breaking ceremony in September 2007, GEO president Wayne Calabrese said that the prison "would give your children and grandchildren a reason to stay and put down roots here in Jena."

Jena mayor Murphy McMillan declared, "This is a great day for Jena."[17]

The Jena Six did not have to look far to see what lay ahead for them.

Justice Warriors

Nothing out of the ordinary happened in Jena in 2006. Black kids were singled out for punishment and railroaded before all-white juries. A small-town prosecutor played god, a role to which he was accustomed. White residents whispered that the black kids had it coming to them. Black parents wrung their hands in impotent frustration as they watched the next generation of black youth begin adulthood with criminal records or in jail. It was business as usual in rural Louisiana.

"So long as these kids were in the dark without representation, they were all going up the river," declared Rev. Jesse Jackson, who traveled to Jena in September 2007. "When the lights came on and the public pressure flooded in, it began to change everything."[18]

It was a movement that was begun around kitchen tables by a group of desperate parents. They have done what they had to, against all odds. A lifetime of racial put-downs and second-class treatment might have worn some down. But in little Jena, Louisiana, picking on the next generation of black youth was one step too far for these tenacious parents and their sons. "You gotta get up, stand up, holler, and fight for your kid," says Bryant Purvis's mother, Tina Jones.

Caseptla Bailey echoes the sentiment. She embodies the slogan from South Africa's anti-apartheid movement: "When you strike a woman, you strike a rock." She gives a hearty laugh of approval at hearing this.

"My advice for other mothers is to stand up and fight," she tells us. "The situation probably feels hopeless in the beginning. I had written a lotta letters to a lotta important agencies for what happened here to my son. So I just continued to hold my head up and continued to write and call. They felt it was just one parent. But once it got past one parent . . . it became a outpouring of the community."

The Jena Six struggle has shone a needed spotlight on hate crimes. Following the civil rights march in Jena in September 2007, fifty to sixty copycat incidents involving nooses in schools and workplaces occurred around the country. It is part of a rising phenomenon: The number of hate crimes in the United States is shockingly high—more than 190,000 incidents per year as of 2005, according to the U.S. Justice Department. The number of hate groups in the United States rose 40 percent from 2000 to 2006, according to the Southern Poverty Law Center.[19]

In December 2007, District Attorney Reed Walters dropped his efforts to try Mychal Bell and agreed to a plea bargain that sharply reduced the charges. Walters dropped a conspiracy charge and agreed to allow Bell to plead guilty to a juvenile charge of second-degree battery. Bell received an eighteen-month sentence in a juvenile prison for his role in the Jena High School fight and several other violations; he received credit for ten months of prison time that he had already served. Bell was released to a foster home several weeks after agreeing to the plea deal. Bell's attorneys say they accepted the deal to spare him the risk of a conviction on more serious charges. Walter offered the plea agreement a week after the *Chicago Tribune* and other media companies won a lawsuit against Judge J. P. Mauffray to force him to open Bell's trial to the public and the press. Bell's deal opened the way for the other members of the Jena Six to strike plea deals with Walters.

Following Congressional hearings into the Jena Six case, members of the Congressional Black Caucus called on Louisiana governor Kathleen Blanco to pardon the six youths. "They and their families have suffered enough, as has the State of Louisiana and the town of Jena," wrote Rep. Sheila Jackson Lee (D-Texas), in a letter signed by fourteen other members of the caucus. Blanco said that she could not issue a pardon without a recommendation from the state Pardon Board, which was not scheduled to meet until after Blanco left office in January 2008.

In late December 2007, eight former and current Jena High School students, white and black, were arrested and charged with setting the fire that destroyed the main wing of their school on November 30, 2006. White residents had openly speculated to us that black students torched the school in retaliation for the noose incident. The eight students who were arrested allegedly burned the school in order to cover up their bad grades and to get out of school. There was apparently no racial motive for the crime.

In spite of their long nightmare, the Jena Six still have big dreams for their futures. Theo Shaw and Robert Bailey, Jr., are determined to finish their education. Theo says, "[I'll] take home school or something. I've got to finish, because I want to go to Grambling [State University in Louisiana]."

Both boys express relief at being free, and amazement that people around the country mobilized around their case. We ask Theo what has surprised him. "That we've got people that are not scared to stand up for what's right."

IV. *Soldiers of* **CONSCIENCE**

Standing Up to the Madness in the 1970s: The GI Movement

They arrived in Vietnam from all parts of America. The conscripts and enlisted men came in the 1960s to defend the world against the tyranny of communism, they were told. But once in Vietnam, American soldiers found themselves part of a military machine in which human rights abuses, indiscriminate killing, and drug addiction were commonplace, and where the local population viewed them as unwanted occupiers. It would become the most unpopular war in the history of the United States.

An organized anti-war movement took root within the military that spread to American bases around the world. The protests took many forms, from soldiers openly participating in antiwar protests, to troops going AWOL, to the proliferation of more than one hundred underground newspapers being published by American soldiers, to outright mutinies on the battlefields. The U.S. Army desertion rate shot up 400 percent between 1966 and 1971, triple the desertion rate of the Korean War. Over a half million soldiers simply vanished, rather than fight an unjust war.

As the documentary film Sir, No Sir! *about the GI Movement recounts: "It was a movement no one expected, least of all those in it.*

Hundreds went to prison and thousands into exile. And by 1971 it had, in the words of one colonel, infested the entire armed services."

Historian Howard Zinn observed in a new edition of Soldiers in Revolt (Haymarket, 2005), the classic history of the GI Movement: "A point can be reached where men and women in uniform can no longer tolerate what they begin to see as an unjust war. It is encouraging to be reminded of the basic desire of human beings to live at peace with other human beings, once they have divested themselves of the deceptions, the nationalism, and the racism that is provoked by war."

CHAPTER 8

Peace Warriors

Augustín Aguayo, a 34-year old Mexican-born army
medic from Southern California, sat in a car with his wife,
Helga, outside a U.S. Army base in Germany. Cars rushed by
outside as Helga filmed her husband of fifteen years on a
video camera. He had spent the previous evening not answer-
ing his phone. He knew his fellow soldiers were calling to try
to convince him to rejoin his unit as they redeployed to Iraq.
"It was just gonna be frustrating for them and frustrating for
me, because in the end, I wasn't gonna go," said Aguayo,
looking tired but determined. His application to be a conscientious objector had just been turned down by the army.
Now he felt he had no choice but to simply refuse to go to
Iraq.

The previous day, September 1, 2006, Aguayo's unit deployed to Iraq; he was not among them. He was now officially absent without leave (AWOL). Aguayo stared directly
into the camera. Brilliant morning sunshine poured into the
small car. The slow-talking, bespectacled soldier addressed
himself to his twin 10-year-old daughters. "Hi Raquel, Hi

Beckie. I love you guys. I miss you guys always when I'm not with you. . . . You guys take care of each other, take care of yourselves. . . . This will be a separation. I don't know what's gonna happen, guys. Soon, we'll be together again."

With that, Augustín Aguayo, dressed in a red T-shirt and loose-fitting jeans, walked into the sprawling base to turn himself in to military police. His crime: refusing to fight in Iraq. Just before passing the main gate, he paused for a moment and turned for a last look at his wife. He looked small and vulnerable, one man against a vast U.S. military machine.

Aguayo's act of conscience was soon to make waves. "I oppose war because I have seen firsthand the direct result of deployments to war zones," he stated in August 2006 to a federal court, explaining why he would not deploy. "As a result of Operation Iraqi Freedom II, I have seen many veterans whose lives have been shattered. Many men came back with missing parts, and countless physical and emotional scars, such as post-traumatic stress disorder. I have personally seen my comrades come back to commit suicide, drink themselves to death, and develop a strong addiction to drugs. It is obvious to me that these men's lives were destroyed by war. What participation in war does to our own soldiers is another reason why war is fundamentally immoral and wrong."

Aguayo knew that refusing to deploy meant he would be court-martialed. But instead of arresting and charging Aguayo the day he turned himself in, army personnel told him flatly that he was going to Iraq, even if they had to shackle him and carry him onto the plane. Soldiers told him to gather his belongings, that he was going to be put on the next flight to the front lines. Two soldiers escorted him back to his apartment, where Helga and his daughters were. They were surprised to see him. When Helga learned that her husband was being sent to Iraq against his will, she began to cry.

Aguayo disappeared into his bedroom to gather his things while the soldiers waited in the living room with Helga and the twins. He rummaged around the house gathering his body armor and uniform. Then he went back into his bedroom to gather more clothes.

Aguayo had to act quickly. "At that moment I realized that my actions, my words weren't enough," he told *Democracy Now!* "It wasn't enough that I was saying, 'I'm against war. I don't believe in this. I can't take part. I won't be a tool of war.'" He looked outside and made his move, jumping out his bedroom window. Then he vanished.

The soldiers sent Helga to find out what was taking her husband so long. They were eager to get Aguayo on a plane. When she went to find him, she saw the bedroom window open. She went back and informed the soldiers simply, "He's gone."

The soldiers were furious. They bolted through the front door and found Aguayo's daughter outside. She began running, and they chased her down the street. "Where's your father? Have you seen him? Where's your father?" they demanded. The little girl burst into tears and ran into the bushes to hide. Helga found her moments later when a neighbor alerted her to what had happened. Helga explained what was going on to her hysterical daughter and calmed her down.

Twenty-six days later, Augustín Aguayo resurfaced in a Los Angeles studio of *Democracy Now!* Dressed in a jacket and tie, but still sporting his military buzz cut, the short, trim man was soft-spoken, even shy. With his mild manner, he seemed more like a librarian than a soldier. But his quiet demeanor belied a steely resolve. He was planning to turn himself in the next day at Fort Irwin in California. But first, he and Helga wanted to talk about what had driven him to resist.

Augustín Aguayo was born in Mexico and grew up in Southern California. He married Helga shortly after high school, and they soon had twin girls. He was working the night shift at a bank to support his family and attending community college during the day when he heard a radio ad for the National Guard. The sales pitch was enticing: work two weeks a year, go away a weekend a month, earn some spare cash, and serve your country. Aguayo spoke to a recruiter, who had just returned from several months in Afghanistan. The soldier told him that deployment was no big deal, and that he mostly read books.

"I was at a crossroads in my life," said Aguayo on *Democracy Now!* "I felt like I had never really done anything for my country. And I saw it also as a way to improve my life. What really appealed to me was the college opportunities."

He enlisted in the army in November 2002. "When I did it, I was very optimistic. . . . I wanted to do good things for my country. I wanted to help people. I wanted positive things in my life. I was eager to become a good soldier."

Aguayo signed up to be a medic. But it was during basic training that he realized he was receiving far more instruction in taking lives than saving them. He would have to carry a rifle, perform guard duty, and go on missions. His unit practiced firing randomly at targets that would appear alongside a road. He recalls being told, "You're a soldier, and you have to be willing and ready to fire, destroy, if necessary."

He began questioning. "Is this right? Is this moral? Is this what God wants?" His doubts led him to make a commitment before going overseas: He would deploy, but he could not take a life.

In February 2004, Aguayo applied to the army for conscientious objector (CO) status. A CO must demonstrate an objection to war in any form, based on a moral or ethical belief. A CO application is a lengthy and difficult process; if it is approved, a soldier is either discharged or transferred to a noncombatant role. While Aguayo was awaiting a decision on his application, his unit was deployed to Iraq. He decided to join his mates in the combat zone, but he would not load his weapon, even while on guard duty.

"It's not my job to decide who's going to live or who's going to die," he told *Democracy Now!* "I won't be a tool of war anymore. The end result of war is the destruction of human life, and governments use that to solve problems. And I think it's a great tragedy of our lifetime, with so much technology, that we still feel that that solves problems."

The investigating officer on Aguayo's CO application found him to be sincere and recommended that his CO application be approved. But the Pentagon, starved for soldiers, was determined to keep Aguayo. His application was turned down in February 2005.

"I felt like they were denying my conscience, like they were telling me, 'No, you're not an objector to war.' I felt that that was like the equivalent of telling someone, 'You're not Catholic' or 'You're not Jewish.'" He informed his superiors that he would continue to look for legal ways to resist.

Aguayo's appeal was denied in August 2006. He was immediately ordered to prepare to return to Iraq with his unit.

But as a true CO, said Helga, "he had no choice but to refuse this war, this deployment."

Defying the authorities has not come easily to Aguayo. "I've always been a great citizen. I've never been in any kind of trouble," he said. "And it's sad that [imprisonment is] going to happen to me, but I feel that in the end I'll be a better person. And I think things happen for a reason. And because of this experience, I can do positive things for others."

Aguayo reflected on the outpouring of support he had received since his case became known. "It's been a wonderful feeling to know that I'm not alone, that many soldiers feel the way I do."

Anti-war resistance has been simmering among the troops since the start of the invasion of Afghanistan in 2001. It is now erupting in every branch of the armed services. The number of conscientious objector applications doubled between 2002 and 2003, when the Iraq invasion began. Officially, the government reports that 425 conscientious objector applications were processed by active and reserve military services between 2002 and 2006; roughly half of these applications, which take an average of seven months to process, were denied.[1] GI rights counselors say the number of CO applications is grossly underreported because the military often finds ways to terminate or make deals with objectors before their cases can be resolved.

Military personnel are now overwhelmingly opposed to the occupation. According to a Le Moyne College/Zogby International poll taken in 2006, 72 percent of American troops serving in Iraq thought the United States should exit the country within a year; more than one in four felt the troops should leave immediately. In a *Military Times* poll in

December 2006, barely one-third of service members approved of the way the president was handling the war.[2]

There are now many signs of resistance within the military. In 2007, the GI Rights Hotline was receiving three to four thousand calls per month from soldiers looking for a way out of the military, up from about one thousand phone calls per month in 2000. J. E. McNeil, an attorney and executive director of the Center on Conscience & War, who works with the GI Rights Hotline, notes that the calls are no longer just from confused young recruits. "Increasingly, we are getting calls from people who have been in the service for ten to eighteen years and are now looking for a way out."

Desertion is spiking. By 2007, soldiers were deserting the army at the highest rate since 1980; there has been an 80 percent increase in the number of deserters since the United States invaded Iraq in 2003.[3] For the first time since the post-Vietnam era, desertion rates exceeded 1 percent of the active duty force in 2000, and are climbing steadily. In 2007, 4,698 soldiers deserted from the U.S. Army, a 42 percent increase over 2006. In an attempt to stop the hemorrhage, the military has cracked down: Since 2002, twice as many soldiers have been court-martialed by the army for desertion and other unauthorized absences than were tried on average each year between 1997 and 2001.[4]

Troops are responding to the "backdoor draft"—in which units, including National Guard and reserves, are being repeatedly deployed for longer and longer stays—with their feet. In a reprise of the Vietnam War rebellion, as many as three hundred military personnel have fled to Canada rather than fight. But the escape route to Canada is closing. In November 2007, the Supreme Court of Canada turned down appeals for official refugee status from Jeremy Hinzman and Brandon Hughey, soldiers who deserted the U.S. Army to protest against the war in Iraq. They face court-martials and up to five years in prison if they are deported to the United States.

The day after his interview with *Democracy Now!* in September 2006, Aguayo gave a press conference. He was surrounded by his parents, his wife and children, members of the clergy, and peace activists. Among the speakers was Fernando Suarez del Solar, father of the first marine from Mexico killed in Iraq. He declared that while he had lost his son Jesus in Iraq, he had another son—Augustín Aguayo.

Helga Aguayo said, "My husband is taking a very courageous step. And I am proud of him."

Augustín Aguayo stepped up to the bank of microphones. Sweat beaded on his forehead as he stood beneath the midday sun, but he appeared at peace with himself. "I never thought I would go AWOL. I never thought I would go to these extremes," he said. "But I felt I had no choice. And because I have taken this stand, I am free, even though my body will probably be locked up for a period of time. It's something I can live with. Something I can't live with is being a participant in war anymore. I don't think it is acceptable to God for humans to destroy each other in this senseless war."

Aguayo continued, "Some people would call me a coward. And I can tell them, I was there, and I did my job. And I was not afraid. And I cannot be there anymore. I cannot support the destruction of life."

With that, Augustín Aguayo and a caravan of supporters drove to Fort Irwin. Dressed in his army camouflage and black beret, he was handcuffed and led onto the base.

Aguayo was soon shipped back to Germany, where he

spent eight months in the brig. Amnesty International recognized him as a conscientious objector and declared him a prisoner of conscience. He was finally released in April 2007 and reunited with his family. He traveled widely in the months following his release to speak about his experience. He continues to speak to students in high schools about alternatives to the military.

In November 2007, Aguayo appealed his case to be recognized as a conscientious objector to the U.S. Supreme Court. Regardless of the legal verdict, his moral stance has been widely recognized: In December 2007, he traveled to Germany to receive the Stuttgart Peace Prize for his unwavering stand in opposing participation in the Iraq War.

He told *Democracy Now!* on his release, "I saved my integrity. I was truly free when I stood up and I finally said, 'I cannot participate anymore, and I'm willing to accept any consequences.'"

Appeal for Redress

Marine Corps Staff Sgt. Liam Madden and a couple of his Marine Corps buddies were looking for a bar while on weekend leave in Norfolk, Virginia, in the fall of 2006. As they walked around, one of them spotted a flier for an anti-war talk. Madden and his friends were Iraq War veterans and all opposed the war. But that was just what they said in bull sessions together. They'd never actually done anything about it, and they certainly never attended an anti-war event. The bar could wait—the three of them wandered into a room in the YWCA to see what was happening. They arrived halfway through a talk being given by David Cortright, a Vietnam veteran, longtime anti-war movement leader, and the author of a history of GI resistance in Vietnam, *Soldiers in Revolt.*

Heads turned as the three marines entered the room. With their buzz cuts and brawn, they "have a presence," Madden concedes. Especially when the rest of the audience is middle-aged peaceniks. Madden was intrigued by Cortright's account of the GI movement in Vietnam, the rebellion among soldiers that spread from the jungles of Vietnam to bases in the United States. GIs created more than 250 anti-war committees and underground newspapers at the height of the uprising, and stories abounded of mutinies and combat refusals.

But Madden felt that it was naïve to imagine that this strategy would catch fire among troops in Iraq. "If that is the hope of the peace movement to end this war, you might wanna reconsider," the compact Marine with bristling black hair piped in during the discussion that followed. He pointed out that Vietnam relied on conscripts, many of whom were in the military against their will. The majority of today's troops signed up for personal and/or economic reasons. To many, it's simply a job. "If you want a person in the military to resist, you are asking them to give up their livelihood and social world."

"We need a better plan," said Madden, not knowing what to suggest. As he headed out into the parking lot afterward, the event's organizer, Navy 3rd Class Petty Officer Jonathan Hutto, caught up with him. "We need to talk," said Hutto. He invited Madden to continue the conversation with him, Cortright, and several other peace activists at the home of a local professor.

"That was a unique experience," Madden recalls. "It was my first anti-war anything." But, he says, "it was not productive."

Over the next few weeks, Madden and Hutto spoke and corresponded. After four years in the military, including a year in Iraq, Madden was disillusioned and pissed off. He was ready to do something to get arrested to show his disgust with the war. But Hutto was intent on finding a legal way for active-duty troops to protest. That's when Hutto came across the Military Whistleblowers Protection Act. It provides a way for active-duty military to communicate their grievances directly to Congress without fear of reprisal.

Hutto and Madden crafted the simple but powerful Appeal for Redress and posted it online in October 2006, followed by an op-ed that Hutto wrote announcing it in the *Navy Times*. The Appeal states:

> As a patriotic American proud to serve the nation in uniform, I respectfully urge my political leaders in Congress to support the prompt withdrawal of all American military forces and bases from Iraq. Staying in Iraq will not work and is not worth the price. It is time for U.S. troops to come home.

The response was stunning: In just a few months, the Appeal garnered more than one thousand signatures. Not since 1969, when 1,366 active-duty service members signed a full-page ad in the *New York Times* demanding an end to the Vietnam War, had there been such a public rebellion by active-duty American armed forces.

Madden and Hutto delivered the Appeal to Congress on Martin Luther King Day in 2007. By late 2007, the Appeal had more than two thousand signatories and was still growing. Among those signing were about three hundred officers, including a number of colonels. About two-thirds were in the army, with 15 percent each from the marines and navy and about 5 percent from the air force. Three-fourths of those signing were active-duty service members. Once a soldier signs the Appeal, it is delivered directly to his or her representatives in Congress, just as a whistleblower would do.

The number of signers may seem small when compared to the 1.4 million people who are in the active-duty U.S. military, and when compared to the 150,000 troops in Iraq. But during the Vietnam War, a time when the United States had 3.5 million soldiers on active duty, the *New York Times* ad drew fewer signatories than the Appeal for Redress garnered in a matter of weeks. And for every signature on the Appeal, organizers estimate there may be hundreds of others who feel similarly but are afraid of possible consequences for speaking out. It is an indicator of the groundswell of discontent within the military that so many have signed on to the Appeal so fast. The Appeal was also helped by the fact that many troops are now aware of the ongoing efforts of anti-war veterans groups, notably Iraq Veterans Against the War (IVAW), Veterans for Peace, and Iraq and Afghanistan Veterans of America.

"The Appeal for Redress is significant in that it is a clear voice from people who are in the military, some of them career people, and they are happy and proud to be in the military—they just object to this war," observes J. E. McNeil of the Center on Conscience & War. "It gives a different feel to it."

Hutto, an African-American who grew up in Atlanta, and Madden, a white man from rural Vermont, took very different journeys to activism. Hutto says his mother's involvement in the civil rights movement deeply influenced him. "I've been political my whole life," he says. "I was raised in a house where political discussions happened every day." Thinking about things politically, he says, is "as natural as having dinner."

Hutto attended Howard University, where he heard former Black Panther leader and Howard alumnus Stokely Carmichael speak. "If you work among the people, the people will never forsake you," Carmichael told the students. Hutto says the speech "profoundly influenced my life."

Hutto immersed himself in student politics. He was elected student body president as a junior and was elected to serve on a Washington, D.C., neighborhood council at the age of 19. A voter registration group that he helped start on campus registered three thousand people. In the fall of 2001, after a Howard alumnus was brutally killed by police, Hutto initiated a police accountability project in Prince George's County, Maryland. After graduation, he went to work doing community outreach for the ACLU, followed by a job running 250 youth chapters for Amnesty International for three years.

But the demands of Hutto's personal life were weighing on him. He had a 3-year-old son, and the long hours of nonprofit work were not compatible with parenting. And he was saddled with $45,000 in student loans. "I knew I wanted to do something to pay off my student loans, give me a decent income, and start my graduate education," he recounts. Then he bumped into a naval officer. "He looked polished," recalls Hutto. More important, the officer said the navy had a program to pay off his student loans. "It got me thinking," says Hutto, "about where I was in my life at that point and how I was needing to get myself together." He was against the war, but gambled that he would probably not be sent to fight in it. In January 2004, Hutto enlisted in the U.S. Navy. He was eventually deployed as a mass communications specialist on the aircraft carrier USS *Theodore Roosevelt* off the coast of Iraq.

Liam Madden did not join the marines fresh out of high school in 2003 in order to make a political statement. We are sitting in the living room of his mother's 150-year-old white farmhouse in southern Vermont. Brilliant fall foliage illuminates each window. His easygoing "aw shucks" charm, chiseled good looks, and eloquence do not suggest a young man who would have trouble making it in the world. But the former high school wrestling team captain says that his choices were stark when he graduated from the nearby high school in Bellow Falls, Vermont: "It was job, jail, college, or military." Madden was a hard partier in high school, which led to several brushes with the law while he was still a student. He felt that he wasn't ready for college. It was his idea to join the marines. "I wanted the personal growth," says the 22-year-old. And, he adds, "I didn't have a way to pay for college."

Madden, whose mom was a local restaurateur and dad was a salesman, finished basic training in January 2003. At the age of 18, he had set himself a challenge and accomplished it. "I was really proud. I did it. I was part of something. I'm a marine now. It's a good first chapter for the book of your life."

Two months after he completed basic training, U.S. forces invaded Iraq. "I heard the drums of war beating and was a little concerned," he concedes. Madden was opposed to attacking Iraq, but he didn't really think it would happen. If the United States did invade, he figured it would be brief, like the month-long Persian Gulf War in 1991, followed by a rapid exit. Madden says he "was appalled that the media and government were in lockstep by manipulating the fear of people and not questioning."

Like Hutto, Madden was a communications specialist. He was initially deployed to Japan, but in September 2004, his unit was sent to Anbar province, the largest province in Iraq and a hotbed of resistance. Anbar includes the cities of Fallujah and Haditha, where he was sent to guard a strategic dam.

What Madden saw in Iraq quickly disabused him of the idea that Americans were being "greeted as liberators," as Vice President Dick Cheney blithely promised in 2003. "People in Iraq had eyes full of fear and hopelessness. It was obvious to me that we were not helping those people. Any help was for propaganda—'Look, we're slapping a coat of paint on a building!' It was not systemic help." He was sent to Fallujah a few months after U.S. forces attacked in retaliation for the killings of four employees of Blackwater, the American mercenary firm. "It was devastated. Just rubble."

Madden alternated between communications work and providing relief to overworked infantrymen. The marines' effort to stem the rising tide of violence was proving futile, and the reality on the ground sharply contradicted the happy talk coming out of Washington about progress that was supposedly being made.

"It was evident to me that we were not helping," Madden recounts. "The resistance was stepping up—every day there were bombs in the road. It was obvious that it was not just a couple of bad guys doing this." Even the language used by the Bush administration and parroted in the media was deceptive. "When you say words like 'insurgent,' 'terrorists,' 'enemy'—it neglects the fact that these are *Iraqis*. The people of Iraq are the resistance!" he exclaims.

Madden's six-month Iraq deployment ended in February 2005. In January 2006, he was stationed in Quantico, Virginia. By then, he was ready for a new fight. "By the time I got to Virginia, I was really excited about the idea that I could do something. I firmly believed that the world needs people to one, step out of their comfort zones. And two," he says, steepling his hands under his chin and paraphrasing Martin Luther King, "if the world is gonna change, it's because people change it. The war is not gonna go away. It's gonna take people doing something. I wanna be part of that."

Jonathan Hutto was also searching for a way to express his deepening opposition to the war. His outrage was intensified by racist incidents on his ship, including having a noose "put in my face by a couple of shipmates." It was around that time that a former professor sent him David Cortright's book *Soldiers in Revolt*, about the Vietnam GI rebellion. "I couldn't put it down," he said. "I was floored by the history."

For Hutto, there is a direct link between his civil rights activism and his approach to organizing in the military. "I really feel that all segments of the population have a right to speak out, a right to be engaged, a right to advocate. No section of the population should be disempowered. And no one is more disempowered than members of the military. Politically, they are trained to be docile," he observes, the passion rising in his voice. "Everyone should have the right to engage in the political process."

When Jonathan Hutto proposed the Appeal for Redress, Madden jumped on it "out of a compulsion to do something."

The two began their efforts in the area they knew best: in their barracks, among friends. It was a clumsy start.

"I knew nothing about organizing at that point," says Madden. So when his fellow marines would gather to watch *Monday Night Football* in the barracks, Madden used the commercial breaks as his organizing moments. "All right everybody, wanna sign this?" he would bellow over the commercials. The result: He got a few signatures, but "was very much ostracized." Hutto and Madden realized they needed some publicity if they were going to reach other service members. David Cortright connected them with a PR firm in Washington. A press conference followed, which led to numerous articles—and the signatures began to flow in.

One signer of the Appeal made a courageous decision to speak to *Democracy Now!* from the front lines in Iraq. Army Sgt. Ronn Cantu, speaking urgently on a crackly phone line, declared, "I'm scared out of my mind right now. . . . All I really want to say—because I shouldn't be doing this—all I want to say is, right now American soldiers are dying in a Sunni-Shiite civil war, a sectarian civil war—that's a fact, based on my personal observations. . . . And it's a belief of the soldiers I've talked to that any troop increase over here, it's just going to be more sitting ducks, more targets."

Liam Madden, who was honorably discharged in January 2007 and is now studying international relations at Northeastern University in Boston, has committed himself to organizing soldiers. He is now president of the Boston chapter of Iraq Veterans Against the War (IVAW). In the summer of 2007, IVAW, which was founded in 2004, launched a campaign encouraging U.S. troops to engage in war resistance. To underscore the point, the group elected Sgt. Camilo Mejia to chair its board of directors. Mejia was the first U.S. combat veteran to publicly refuse to redeploy to Iraq. He went underground and then served nearly a year in a jail.

Madden, who serves on the IVAW board of directors, explains, "Soldiers' resistance has to be a focal point. Organizing collective action from within the ranks is gonna be what ends this war."

In the course of our conversation, Madden stops to do a brief radio interview. He is asked his view of his commander in chief and of Vice President Cheney. "I personally believe they are war criminals," he says without hesitating. Sounding like a seasoned media professional, he is quick on his feet and forceful. "They committed a war of aggression. Certainly they should be impeached for trampling on the Constitution."

The reporter peppers him: "You signed up for the marines and promised to follow orders and fight. What did you expect?"

"No one signs up to be lied to," Madden fires back. He paces the room as he talks. "No one signs up to put their life on the line for lies and oil. Yeah, we need to figure out what's best for the Iraqi people. If [Bush] thinks that 90 percent of the Iraqi population that wants the U.S. occupation to end doesn't know what's best for them, then who are we to impose what's best for them?"

Madden's frequent and forceful public statements have caught the attention of the military. In the spring of 2007, he received a letter from the marines threatening to revoke his honorable discharge. Madden tossed the grenade right back.

"Sir, is honesty disloyalty?" he wrote to the colonel who sent him a threatening letter. He concluded his letter pointedly, "I understand men in your position have their careers to think about, as I'm positive many German colonels did in

1939." He signed off, "Semper Fidelis"—always faithful. The Marine Corps motto signifies the loyalty that marines are expected to demonstrate even after leaving the service. The marines backed off.

"I am glad I was a marine," says Madden, explaining the thinking behind his tough response to his former bosses. "However, I have deep concerns with how marines are indoctrinated and employed."

Appeal for Redress has been hailed in *The Nation* as "the most significant movement of organized and dissident GIs seen in America," and attacked in *The Atlantic Monthly* as "short-sighted and dangerous" and "likely to warp national-security policy."[5] Madden took issue with the latter, responding in an unpublished letter, "The Appeal for Redress is not the military seeking a more prominent role in politics; it is in fact troops renouncing the role being projected onto them."

Liam's mother, Oona, walks into the room as her son is talking. She knows her son has been giving numerous interviews—Liam is thumbing through the current issue of *The Commons,* an independent Vermont newspaper, that features a full-page front-cover photo of him under the headline, "The Making of a Maverick"—but she's never been interviewed herself. We ask her a few questions. What does she think of President Bush?

"I think Bush is an honest man. He may be ineffective. He may have made some bad choices. But I think his heart is in the right place."

Does she feel the government lied about the reasons for going to war? "No, I don't. I think there are people in government who are ill informed."

Did she ever imagine Liam would be doing what he is

doing today? "Not in a million years!" she says with a chuckle. She adds, "I'm very proud and very supportive of Liam and what he's doing. Because I think it is hugely important for people to make waves when they feel strongly about things they feel are wrong. Nothing would ever have changed in this country if people didn't say, 'Hey, this is not right.'"

Liam listens without challenging his mother, then gives her a bear hug as she stands to leave. Afterward, he just shrugs. He says his mom's perspective "makes my views stronger, because I encounter other good solid points. But yeah," he says with a smile, "it's a little frustrating."

What gives this anti-war marine hope? "My generation are so bright, so talented, so fun—*they* give me a lot of hope. And history gives me a lot of hope—Eugene Debs, Martin Luther King—people who sought to change the world. I disagree with a lot of things Malcolm X said, but he's a hero in how he defied conventional thinking. Learning from history—that gives me hope.

"I think people are the solution. Organization is the solution," he says. "We need a revolution of conscience. And it needs to be well organized."

Hutto, whose navy commitment runs until 2010, sees the Appeal for Redress as part of a larger effort. "Long-term, we want to build a permanent advocacy engine for folks in the military. Not only around issues of war, but also to advocate on grievances that members of the military have, from the way veterans are treated, to health care they receive, to the stress their families endure." He also hopes to address the issues he faced "around racism, sexism, homophobia, and low tolerance in general." He has written a book about his experiences, *Antiwar Soldier*.

This modern soldier's revolt is getting recognition for its significance in the larger social justice movement. On October 17, 2007, Madden and Hutto traveled to Washington, D.C., to receive the annual Letelier-Moffit Human Rights Award from the Institute for Policy Studies. The award is named for two murdered human rights activists, Chilean diplomat Orlando Letelier and American Ronni Karpen Moffitt. "That was a proud moment for us," Hutto tells us. "We took pride in knowing we are not alone, that there are people out there who are willing to help and aid us and push this movement forward." They used the occasion to release another thousand grievances from military personnel who signed the Appeal.

Madden has a word of encouragement for lonely activists involved in quixotic struggles. "I'm involved in this because someone saw a flier. Don't discount your efforts if you think that your little event is worthless. Because someone saw a flier, it brought in two thousand names of soldiers. That should inspire people."

An Officer Objects

By 2006, dissent among the troops was widespread. Even high-ranking military officials, in what became known as the Generals' Revolt, were openly criticizing the Bush administration—once the officers had retired. But no active-duty officer had yet broken ranks. An army lieutenant was about to change all that.

On June 6, 2006, U.S. Army 1st Lt. Ehren Watada, dressed in a business suit and standing before a U.S. flag, issued a video statement in which he announced that he would refuse to deploy to Iraq. He was supposed to make his announcement at a news conference, but military officials warned Watada that he could not speak publicly while on duty at the base.

Watada is the first commissioned officer to refuse service. In a slow, measured tone that dramatized the gravitas of his action, Watada declared:

It is my duty as a commissioned officer of the United States Army to speak out against grave injustices. My moral and legal obligation is to the Constitution and not to those who would issue unlawful orders. I stand before you today because it is my job to serve and protect America's soldiers, as people, and innocent Iraqis who have no voice. It is my conclusion as an officer of the armed forces that the war in Iraq is not only morally wrong, but a horrible breach of American law.

Although I've tried to resign out of protest, I will be forced to participate in a war that is manifestly illegal. As the order to take part in an illegal act is ultimately unlawful as well, I must, as an officer of honor and integrity, refuse that order.

The war in Iraq violates our democratic system of checks and balances. It usurps international treaties and conventions that, by virtue of the Constitution, become American law. The wholesale slaughter and mistreatment of Iraqis is not only a terrible, moral injustice, but it is a contradiction to the army's own Law of Land Warfare. My participation would make me party to war crimes. Normally, those in the military have allowed others to speak for them and act on their behalf. I believe that time has come to an end.

Lieutenant Watada's defiance sent shock waves through the military. He had joined the service in March 2003, believing President Bush's claims that Saddam Hussein had weapons of mass destruction and connections to 9/11 and al-Qaeda, and that Iraq was an imminent threat to the United States. He joined "out of a desire to protect our country."

Watada wanted to be the best kind of officer. He wanted to learn about the country and culture he thought he was being sent to defend. That's when rhetoric and reality began to part ways. "In my preparation for deployment to Iraq, in order to better train myself and my soldiers, I began to research the background of Iraq, including the culture, the history, the events going on on the ground, and what had led us up into the war in the first place," he told *Democracy Now!* "What I found was very shocking to me and dismaying, and it really made me question what I was being asked to do. . . . I became convinced that the war itself was illegal and immoral, as was the current conduct of American forces and the American government on the ground over in Iraq."

The lieutenant took his role in the army—and the war—seriously. As an officer, he had to lead troops in battle. "I just felt that the policies that were made were forcing soldiers, including myself, to commit actions that violated international and domestic laws."

In January 2006, Lieutenant Watada requested to resign his commission and leave the military. The army denied his request and gave him an ultimatum: deploy to Iraq or face a court-martial. That's when the earnest, clean-cut lieutenant went on the attack, becoming the first officer to publicly refuse service in Iraq. And he went further, charging publicly that the war in Iraq was illegal and immoral.

Ehren Watada was born in Hawaii in 1978 to Japanese-American parents. His father, Robert, a retired Hawaiian state official, refused to serve in the Vietnam War and instead joined the Peace Corps and worked in Peru.

Ehren's mother, Carolyn Ho, struggled with her son's decision to refuse deployment to Iraq. She recounted on *Democracy Now!* that when her son called to tell her what he was doing, "We got into a huge, huge fight on the phone. And I said, '. . . Do you realize what is going to happen? You're one little lieutenant facing the huge military-industrial complex. . . . Why can you not just finish off your tour of duty and just put it behind you, and then you will go on with your life?'" Then she hung up on him. She was distraught, but later recalled a poem by Khalil Gibran. "It's about our children, and that they come through us, but they don't belong to us. . . . I realized that beyond trying to protect him, I needed to support his decision."

Carolyn Ho called her son back. Ehren told her, "For me, this is a matter of conscience, and you were asking me to betray my conscience. I can't do that." He added, "You've always taught me to do the right thing. So why are you asking me now not to do the right thing?"

Ehren added, "I would rather languish in prison than be responsible for the deaths of my soldiers, and be responsible for their committing war crimes . . . in this illegal war."

"For me," said Ho, her son's act of conscience "has been the first step in a journey of a thousand miles." She realized, "What is life if you cannot live with your conscience?"

"I totally support him," Ho says now. "And I will continue to speak out until justice is served."

Watada's actions seemed to be right in line with the

views of Gen. Peter Pace. In 2006, the chairman of the Joint Chiefs of Staff declared, "It is the absolute responsibility of everybody in uniform to disobey an order that is either illegal or immoral."

But when Watada went public with his refusal, the military went ballistic. Military prosecutors not only charged Watada with failing to report for duty, but for the first time in forty-one years, the military charged someone with "conduct unbecoming an officer" for his public statements. And in an unprecedented move, the army subpoenaed journalists in order to make its case that Watada publicly criticized the president and the military. After protests from journalists, the military later dropped its demand that reporters testify.

If there really were justice in our society, who would be charged with "conduct unbecoming": The commander in chief who launched an illegal war, sending thousands of soldiers to kill and be killed? Or the first brave army officer to publicly speak truth to power and resist such an order?

Watada's first court-martial, at which the judge prevented him from introducing evidence of the war's illegality, ended in a mistrial in February 2007. The army refiled charges, but Watada's lawyers claimed he was facing double jeopardy—being illegally tried for the same crime twice. In November 2007, U.S. District Court Judge Benjamin Settle issued a preliminary injunction in Watada's favor, ruling that the military judge "abused his discretion" in declaring a mistrial. Settle ordered that the army cannot hold a second court-martial until the federal court resolves the double jeopardy claim.

In defying the military, Watada insists he is acting in the highest traditions of military behavior. "I love my country," he told *Democracy Now!* "And I believe in our principles of democracy. We're ruled by the people and equality for all. I know I would do anything it takes to ensure that that prevails."

Watada's defiance stirred up old divisions within the Japanese-American community. Watada was at first criticized by some Japanese-American World War II veterans, who fought for the United States despite the fact that 120,000 Japanese-Americans were stripped of their civil rights and interred in American concentration camps during the war. But Watada was embraced by the No-No Boys—the Japanese-Americans who refused to serve in World War II.

Watada decided to try to bridge this half-century-old divide by speaking to veterans on both sides. He told them, "It doesn't matter what one believes the intent of the other was, or if one group was right or the other was wrong. Both groups were trying to prove to America that, even though they were Japanese-Americans, they were still Americans."

Hawaii Sen. Daniel Akaka, whose grandson is serving in Iraq, expressed his support for Watada on *Democracy Now!* "I admire his position," he said. "It's a position that has grown with him being reared and brought up in Hawaii in a diverse population and with diverse culture and a care for people. And what he has done is so difficult, for any young man to take a position like that, to the point where he is willing to resign as an officer and to leave the service of the United States. But he bases it on the mistakes that this country has made. And so, he needs to be admired for that."

Ehren Watada took a lonely, courageous stand that inspired countless others. He said he receives word from service members each day who draw strength from his action. We asked him what gives him strength to do what he has done.

"The opportunity to make a difference," he replied. "I see the path that our country is taking is so wrong and so destructive, all from the conduct and the ideology of our leadership. And I just think anything I can do to put a stop to this, to make things right, I'll do it."

CONCLUSION

"We Are the Leaders We Have Been Waiting For"

People often ask us in our travels, "What gives you hope?"

"You do," we reply time and again. The people and movements we write about in this book—and the countless deserving activists who are not chronicled here—are the reason why.

Protesting is an act of love. It is born of a deeply held conviction that the world can be a better, kinder place. Saying "no" to injustice is the ultimate declaration of hope.

But the corporate media ignores and ridicules grassroots activists who speak out. Concerned citizens are thus left wondering: Where are the millions marching in the streets to defend human rights, civil liberties, and racial justice? Where is the mass revulsion against the killing and torture being carried out in our name? Where are the environmentalists? Where is the peace movement?

The answer, as we found in our journeys around the country, is that activists and peacemakers are everywhere. And they are changing how politics is done.

The issues of war, peace, torture, privacy, censorship, global warming, racism, and justice—to name but a few of today's burning concerns—have penetrated deep into the fabric of our society. The Bush administration has kept a nation spellbound and cowed by using the threat of what Franklin Roosevelt called "nameless, unreasoning, unjustified terror."

But this government crackdown has boomeranged. Suddenly, the battlefronts in this war *of* terror are not just in foreign deserts. There is now a war on dissent, and the battle lines are in our communities: Our libraries, schools, neighborhoods, and homes have become contested terrain. Assaulting civil liberties serves a vital political purpose for a rogue administration that lacks popular support: When dissenters are muzzled and smeared, potential adversaries are intimidated into silence. This has been a fateful overreaching by a government obsessed with maintaining power by any means necessary.

Wherever there is injustice, there is resistance. It may not begin as mass protest, but it often ends up that way. We have found people from all walks of life taking stands right where they are:

- A lone soldier inside a vast military base refusing to fight.
- A librarian standing toe-to-toe with FBI agents, declining to name names of library patrons.
- A man wearing an Arabic peace T-shirt standing up to racial profiling.
- Another man in dreadlocks in a flooded and abandoned African-American neighborhood of New Orleans

hanging sheetrock, restoring life to a forsaken neighborhood, house by house.

- High school students from Connecticut performing a play about soldiers in Iraq at theaters in New York City, after being banned and shunned by their own school.

From Louisiana to Connecticut to California to Iraq, we were moved by the courage and dignity shown by ordinary people in these extraordinary times. Acting on one's conscience has entailed risk for everyone we met. Drama teacher Bonnie Dickinson risked losing her job. Conscientious objector Augustín Aguayo faced jail and separation from his wife and young daughters. Malik Rahim had to fear for his life as he confronted vigilantes in New Orleans. Psychologist Jean Maria Arrigo contemplated being ostracized by her profession. Six Jena High School students faced lives in prison instead of a future of promise.

In each instance, individuals had to take a leap of faith. They could only hope that if they led, others would follow. That is how movements are born. What begins as one, eventually becomes many.

The Connecticut librarians discovered this when they watched their terrorism trial through closed circuit TV and saw a courtroom filled with librarians who had come in solidarity.

Psychologists against torture turned out in the hundreds to demand that their colleagues—and the American Psychological Association—act as healers, not tormentors.

And the principled resistance of climate scientists was inspired by and catalyzed global warming activists to ratchet up their struggle to save our planet.

War resisters such as Army Spc. Augustín Aguayo and Lt

Ehren Watada learned they were not alone when hundreds turned out to support them as they took their courageous stands against participating in a murderous and illegal war.

Navy Seaman Jonathan Hutto and Marine Sgt. Liam Madden bravely made an Appeal for Redress, and two thousand service members joined them.

How to Stand Up to the Madness

Stopping the madness begins with a single act of resistance. The experiences of the people and movements we have profiled hold lessons that we can take into our own communities, wherever we are and whatever the issue.

1. CHALLENGE THE CORPORATE MEDIA

Instead of waiting for the corporate media to cover us, we can make our own media and communicate in our own words with our communities, and the world.

HOW YOU CAN TAKE ACTION

- *Support independent media.* For true democracy to work, people need easy access to independent, diverse sources of news and information. For millions of listeners and viewers, that news source is *Democracy Now!* (democracynow.org), a daily grassroots, global, unembedded, international, independent news hour. Launched in 1996, *Democracy Now!* features people and perspectives rarely heard in the U.S. corporate-sponsored media, including independent and international journalists, ordinary people from around the world who are directly affected by U.S. foreign policy, grassroots leaders and peace activists, artists, academics, and independent analysts. *Democracy Now!* has pioneered the largest public media collaboration in the United States. It is broadcast on Pacifica, NPR, community, and college radio stations; on public access and PBS television stations, and both satellite television networks (DISH network: Free Speech TV channel 9415 and Link TV channel 9410; DirecTV: Link TV channel 375); and on the Internet. The video and audio podcast of *Democracy Now!* is one of the most popular on the Web. Every week, a new public radio or television station begins airing *Democracy Now!* Get your local radio or television station to carry the show (find organizing information at democracynow.org or call 888-999-3877). Tune in. Hear the voices of the silenced majority. And spread the word.

- *Create your own media.* The independent media movement, which gained prominence in 1999 by providing grassroots coverage of the World Trade Organization protests in Seattle, has gone global. Post your own stories, photos, and media at **indymedia.org**. Become active in your local community radio station. **Pacifica Radio** (pacifica.org) was founded in 1949 as the first noncommercial independent radio network and grew to five listener-funded stations; check for affiliates in your area. Volunteer. Become involved in your local public access TV station and fight to preserve local control of public, educational, and government television (ourchannels.org).
- *Stop big media.* The Democratic and Republican par-

ties have empowered the Federal Communications Commission to enable the half-dozen giant companies that own most of the media in the United States to gobble up even more media outlets. If you value local ownership and want a diversity of voices in your news, become active in the national **media reform movement,** including the **Media Action Grassroots Network** (mediagrassroots.org) and **Free Press** (free press.net).

• *Save Net neutrality.* The Internet should be free and open for everyone. Net neutrality prevents Internet providers from speeding up or slowing down Web content based on its source, ownership or destination. Tell your Congressional representatives to stop the big telephone and cable companies from becoming over-lords of the Internet, deciding which Web sites load fast, slow, or not at all. Learn more at **Savetheinter net.com.**

2. DON'T FOLLOW THE LEADERS

Psychologist Jean Maria Arrigo broke with the American Psychological Association when she realized that her colleagues who cooperate with torture undermine an entire healing profession. She told us, "I didn't want to be that person who couldn't make a small move because it would hurt a little bit."

HOW YOU CAN TAKE ACTION

• *Stop torture.* From Guantánamo Bay to the casual use of Tasers by police, torture must be confronted everywhere, by everyone.

Psychologists determined to stop torture teamed up with **Physicians for Human Rights** (physicians forhumanrights.org) to organize and make their case. PHR is a twenty-year-old organization that works with health care professionals to advance social justice and human rights. For more information about how psychologists are fighting torture, visit ethicalapa.com and psychoanalystsopposewar.org/blog.

The **Center for Constitutional Rights** (ccrjustice .org) has been a leader in the legal campaign to stop torture and protect human rights. CCR brought the first Guantánamo case to court, and it represents numerous other Guantánamo prisoners. Founded in 1966 by attorneys who represented civil rights activists in the South, CCR has a long history of working closely with grassroots groups on issues ranging from human rights to racial justice, voting rights, and civil liberties.

3. QUESTION AUTHORITY

For the peace warriors within the military, questioning authority—a fundamental break with military ethos—was the beginning of their journey away from war and death to a just and peaceful tomorrow.

HOW YOU CAN TAKE ACTION

- *Support the troops—bring them home.* Stop the lying. Stop the dying. Bring the troops home now. That's what the overwhelming majority of active duty military personnel say they want.

Soldiers of conscience face a lonely fight. They are in every community, and they need information and support. The **GI Rights Hotline** (800-394-9544 or 877-447-4487, girights@objector.org) is a first stop for service members and their families who need information about military discharges and other civil rights issues.

Other organizations that provide information and advice about conscientious objection, draft registration, and countering the militarization of schools include: the **Central Committee for Conscientious Objectors** (objector.org, which includes an extensive list of links to other anti-war organizations), the **Center on Conscience & War** (centeronconscience.org), and **American Friends Service Committee** (afsc.org).

Many active duty soldiers, veterans, and military families are working for peace with **Iraq Veterans Against the War** (ivaw.org), **Veterans for Peace** (veteransforpeace.org), and **Military Families Speak Out** (mfso.org).

To learn about the little known story of GI resistance during the Vietnam War, see the documentary film *Sir, No Sir!* (sirnosir.com).

4. SPEAK UP

When climate scientist James Hansen defied the censors, he spoke for the silenced majority: other scientists and the public who had been silenced by Big Oil and its junk scientists and the corporate media who have acted as a megaphone for their fictions. By speaking out, he emboldened and helped catalyze the movement to stop global warming.

- *Stop global warming.* The personal is political: Don't preach to others until you reduce your own carbon footprint (smaller homes, energy-efficient appliances and lighting are in; paramilitary-style vehicles that get less than 30 mpg are out). Then work with groups helping to wage the political battle to fight global warming.

  The 1Sky Campaign (1sky.org), launched in the fall of 2007, is spearheading a coordinated effort to stop climate change. 1Sky calls for creating 5 million new "green jobs" in the United States to help communities conserve 20 percent of their energy use by 2015; cut global warming pollution 30 percent by 2020 and at least 80 percent by 2050; and declare a moratorium on new coal plants and invest in renewable energy. 1Sky is a diverse coalition that includes Step It Up, Sierra Club, U.S. Public Interest Research Group, Natural Resources Defense Council, Ella Baker Center for Human Rights, scientists such as Dr. James Hansen, and numerous others. The **U.S. Climate Emergency Council** (climateemergency.org), part of the 1Sky Campaign, works on grassroots mobilization to stop global warming.

5. SAY NO

The edifice of the draconian USA PATRIOT Act cracked when two FBI agents encountered a librarian in Connecticut who responded with the most powerful word in our language:

No. We will not be participants in deceiving the public. We will not betray the trust of those we serve. We will not cooperate in tyranny.

HOW YOU CAN TAKE ACTION

- *Defend your rights.* Bullies—and governments who act like them—are only as powerful as their adversaries allow them to be. Push back against intimidation and repression. Recruit allies.

  When the FBI confronted librarians, the librarians turned for help to the **American Civil Liberties Union** (aclu.org). Founded in 1920, the organization has offices in almost every state and handles nearly 6,000 cases per year defending basic rights and liberties guaranteed in the U.S. Constitution. The librarians' bold stand earned them the 2006 ACLU Roger Baldwin Medal of Liberty. The award is named for the founder of the ACLU, who said, "So long as we have enough people in this country willing to fight for their rights, we'll be called a democracy."

  Make your community a free speech zone. Organize a local resolution to protect civil liberties, an effort being led by the Bill of Rights Defense Committee (bordc.org).

- *Protect libraries.* Public libraries are a cornerstone of democracy. They are part of the public commons, a sanctuary for the free exchange of information and ideas. But they are under threat. From book banning to government surveillance, libraries have been a target in the "war on terror." The **American Library Association** (ala.org), founded in 1876, works "to enhance learning and ensure access to information for all." It has been a staunch defender of public libraries and the rights of patrons to access information without fear of retribution.

6. STAND TOGETHER

When Jim Crow justice reared its head to claim a new generation of victims in Jena, Louisiana, a group of African-American youths and families stood together to fight back. Their brave stand has galvanized a nationwide movement. In New Orleans, public housing activists have shined a light on how racism burns on—and must be challenged.

HOW YOU CAN TAKE ACTION

- *Confront racism.* The outrage of what happened to the Jena Six was just a local matter until the case was noticed and publicized by outsiders. One of the first groups to take an interest was **Friends of Justice** (friendsofjustice.wordpress.com), which formed in response to the notorious roundup and incarceration of African-American residents of the small town of Tulia, Texas, in 1999. The group organizes in poor communities across Texas and Louisiana to demand fair and equal justice. The Jena Six case has involved numerous other groups working on racial justice, including the **ACLU** and **NAACP** (naacp.org). For more information on the school-to-prison pipeline, see the **Sentencing Project** (sentencingproject.org) and the **Advancement Project** (advancementproject.org).
- *Help rebuild New Orleans.* The residents of New Orleans are in a desperate fight for survival. Some of the

grassroots groups trying to defend the right to return for residents following Hurricane Katrina include: **Common Ground Relief** (commongroundrelief.org) and **People's Hurricane Relief Fund** (peopleshurricane.org).

7. TAKE THE SHOW ON THE ROAD

By standing up in Connecticut, high school students and their courageous teacher brought the voices of soldiers on the front lines to a national stage. They would not be complicit in silencing the voices of dissent.

HOW YOU CAN TAKE ACTION

- *Fight censorship.* Controversial art, drama, and books should be debated, not banned. The **National Coalition Against Censorship** (ncac.org), which gave its 2007 annual award to the student actors of Wilton High School for standing up to censorship, has been a leader in protecting the free expression of ideas.

Ordinary heroes teach us that democracy can, and must, be defended everywhere, by everyone. "We are the leaders we have been waiting for," has become a rallying cry of the climate change movement. This spirit of resistance has the power to save our democracy, and our world.

The German students of the White Rose warned in their first leaflet: "It is certain that today every honest German is ashamed of his government. Who among us has any conception of the dimensions of shame that will befall us and our children when one day the veil has fallen from our eyes and the most horrible of crimes . . . reach the light of day?"

That veil has long since fallen in America. The crimes—racist arrests, war, illegal surveillance, torture, roundup of immigrants, to name a few—are happening in plain sight. These violations will not simply stop with a change in leadership in Washington—unless we force an end to the crimes and the criminals. Democrats and Republicans alike have been served notice that lip service and deception will not satisfy the new generation of activists that is demanding real change and real democracy.

Now more than ever, it is imperative that we defend our liberties. Speak truth to power. Fight for those who can't. Demand peace, and end the bloodshed. And save our struggling planet.

Now more than ever—and always—we must stand up to the madness.

Notes

INTRODUCTION

1. Joby Warrick and Dan Eggen, "Hill Briefed on Waterboarding," *Washington Post*, December 9, 2007.

1. RECLAIMING COMMON GROUND

1. Reprinted with permission of Sunni Patterson.
2. Nikki Davis Maute, "Power Crews Diverted; Restoring Pipeline Came First," *Hattiesburg American,* September 11, 2005. www.newsdesk.org/archives/003447.html
3. "Lower Ninth Ward Community Snapshot," Greater New Orleans Community Data Center. http://www.gnocdc.org/orleans/8/22/snapshot.html
4. "After the Flood," *The Nation,* September 10, 2007.
5. Courtney Mabeus, "The Ties That Bind," *Capital Eye,* Center for Responsive Politics, October 13, 2007.
6. Ibid.
7. Jenny Bergal and John Perry, "Katrina Contracts Worth $2.4 Billion Offer Profit Guarantees," *Katrina Watch,* Center for Public Integrity, June 21, 2007. www.publicintegrity.org/Katrina/Report.aspx?aid=882
8. Courtney Mabeus, "The Ties That Bind," *Capital Eye,* Center for Responsive Politics, October 13, 2007.

9. Michael Tisserand, "The Charter School Flood," *The Nation,* September 10, 2007.

10. *Democracy Now!,* August 30, 2007.

11. Susan Saulny, "New Orleans Hurt by Acute Rental Shortage," *New York Times,* December 3, 2007.

12. Charles Babington, "Some GOP Legislators Hit Jarring Notes in Addressing Katrina," *Washington Post*, September 10, 2005.

13. Adam Nossiter, "Whites Take a Majority in New Orleans Council," *New York Times,* November 20, 2007.

14. Cain Burdeau, "New Orleans Fracas Over Plans to Raze Housing," Associated Press, December 6, 2007.

2. T IS FOR TERRORIST

1. *Sanctioned Bias: Racial Profiling Since 9/11,* ACLU, February 2004, p. 4.

2. David Cole, "Are We Safer?" *New York Review of Books*, March 9, 2006.

3. Donna Leinwand, "Black Drivers Searched More Often, Feds Say; Disparities Appear after Initial Stop," *USA Today,* April 30, 2007.

4. "Racial Profiling Fact Sheet," ACLU, November 23, 2005. aclu.org/racialjustice/racialprofiling/21741res20051123.html

5. "FBI Apologizes to Lawyer in Bombing Case," *Associated Press,* May 25, 2004.

6. William McCall, "2 Patriot Act Provisions Ruled Unlawful," *Associated Press,* September 27, 2007.

7. Robert L. Jamieson, Jr., "Inflaming Fears Doesn't Make Anyone Safe," *Seattle Post-Intelligencer,* August 28, 2007.

8. *Democracy Now!,* September 1, 2006.

9. Matthew Rothschild, "Two Rows Over a T-shirt with Arabic on It," *The Progressive*, October 25, 2006.

3. LIBRARIANS UNBOUND

1. "A Review of the FBI's Use of National Security Letters," Office of the Inspector General, U.S. Department of Justice, March 2007, p. 62. http://www.usdoj.gov/oig/special/s0703b/final.pdf

2. "Ashcroft Says FBI Hasn't Used PATRIOT Act Library Provision, Mocks ALA for 'Hysteria,'" *ALA Online,* September 23,

2003. ala.org/ala/alonline/currentnews/newsarchive/2003/sep
tember2003/ashcroftsays.cfm

3. Michael B. Mukasey, "The Spirit of Liberty," *Wall Street Journal*,
May 10, 2004.

4. Alison Leigh Cowan, "Connecticut Librarians See Lack of Oversight as Biggest Danger in Antiterror Law," *New York Times*,
September 3, 2005.

5. Ibid.

6. Jane Gordon, "In Patriots' Cradle, the PATRIOT Act Faces
Scrutiny," *New York Times*, April 24, 2005.

7. "Testimony of ACLU Client and National Security Letter
Recipient George Christian at a Hearing of the Senate Judiciary Subcommittee on the Constitution," ACLU, April 11,
2007. http://www.aclu.org/safefree/general/293081eg200704
11.html

8. Alison Leigh Cowan, "A Court Fight to Keep a Secret
That's No Real Secret at All," *New York Times*, November 18,
2005.

9. *Doe v. Gonzales*, "Opinion and Decision Order," U.S. District
Court, Southern District, September 6, 2007. http://www.aclu
.org/pdfs/safefree/nsldecisio.pdf

4. SOME DON'T LIKE IT HOT

1. Andrew Revkin, "NASA Chief Backs Agency Openness," *New
York Times*, February 4, 2006.

2. Andrew Revkin, "NASA's Goals Delete Mention of Home
Planet," *New York Times*, July 22, 2006.

3. John Vidal, "Revealed: How Oil Giant Influenced Bush," *The
Guardian* (UK), June 8, 2005.

4. *Atmosphere of Pressure*, Union of Concerned Scientists & Government Accountability Project, January 2007, p. 2.

5. Editorial, "Doubting Inhofe," *New York Times*, October 12, 2006.

6. Editorials, *Investor's Business Daily:* "The 'Old' Consensus?,"
September 27, 2007; "Chilling Effect," August 7, 2007.

7. The Heinz Awards, www.heinzawards.net.

8. Andrew Revkin, "NASA's Chief Backs Agency Openness," *New
York Times*, February 4, 2006.

9. Andrew Revkin, "Climate Expert Says NASA Tried to Silence
Him," *New York Times*, January 29, 2006.

10. Ibid.
11. *Climate Change 2001: Summary for Policymakers,* Intergovernmental Panel on Climate Change, p. 9. http://www.ipcc.ch/pub/SYRspm.pdf
12. "ExxonMobil's Continued Funding of the Global Warming Denial Industry," Greenpeace, May 2007. http://www.greenpeace.org/usa/assets/binaries/exxon-secrets-analysis-of-fun
13. Andrew Revkin, "A Young Bush Appointee Resigns His Post at NASA," *New York Times,* February 8, 2006.
14. "Press Briefing by Dana Perino," Office of the Press Secretary, The White House, October 24, 2007.
15. Julie Eilperin, "Bush Aide Rejects Climate Goal," *Washington Post*, October 19, 2007.
16. Greenpeace, May 2007, p. 4.
17. Jennifer Washburn, "The Best Minds Money Can Buy," *Los Angeles Times,* July 21, 2006.
18. Jennifer Washburn, "Big Oil Buys Berkeley," *Los Angeles Times,* March 25, 2007.
19. Charles Burress, "40 Protest UC Berkeley Research Deal with BP," *San Francisco Chronicle,* October 5, 2007.
20. Jennifer Washburn, "Big Oil Buys Berkeley," *Los Angeles Times,* March 25, 2007.
21. *Democracy Now!,* September 6, 2007.

5. PSYCHOLOGISTS IN DENIAL

1. "U.S. Detains Nearly 25,000 in Iraq," Agence France-Presse, October 10, 2007.
2. *Democracy Now!,* February 17, 2006.
3. Office of the Inspector General, *Review of DoD-Directed Investigations of Detainee Abuse,* Department of Defense, August 26, 2006. http://www.fas.org/irp/agency/dod/abuse.pdf
4. Neil Lewis, "Red Cross Finds Detainee Abuse in Guantánamo," *New York Times,* November 30, 2004.
5. Adam Zagorin, Michael Duffy, "Inside the Interrogation of Detainee 063," *Time,* June 12, 2005.
6. M. G. Bloche and J. H. Marks, "Doctors and Interrogators at Guantánamo Bay," *New England Journal of Medicine* 353:6–8, July 7, 2005.
7. Ibid.

8. Adam Zagorin, "'20th Hijacker' Claims That Torture Made Him Lie," *Time,* Friday, March 03, 2006.

9. Bill Dedman, "Aggressive Interrogation at Guantánamo May Prevent His Prosecution," MSNBC.com, October 26, 2006.

10. *Democracy Now!*, July 30, 2007.

11. Katherine Eban, "Rorschach and Awe," vanityfair.com, July 17, 2007.

12. Petula Dvorak, "Fort Hunt's Quiet Men Break Silence on WWII," *Washington Post*, October 6, 2007.

13. Scott Shane, David Johnston, and James Risen, "Secret U.S. Endorsement of Severe Interrogations," *New York Times,* October 4, 2007.

14. Andrew Sullivan, "Bush's Torturers Follow Where the Nazis Led," *Sunday Times* (London), October 7, 2007.

15. Jane Mayer, "The Experiment," *The New Yorker,* July 11, 2005.

16. Steven Reisner, et al., "Open Letter to Sharon Brehm," June 7, 2007. http://psychoanalystsopposewar.org/blog/wp-content/uploads/2007/06/openlettertosharonbrehmfinalnp.pdf

17. "Presidential Task Force on Psychological Ethics and National Security: 2003 Members' Biographical Statements," American Psychological Association.

18. Ibid.

19. Mark Benjamin, "Psychological Warfare," Salon.com, July 26, 2006.

20. Reisner, et al.

21. Open letter from Col. Larry James to APA president Sharon Brehm, June 18, 2007. http://psychoanalystsopposewar.org/blog/wp-content/uploads/2007/06/larryjameslettertoapapresidentdrsharonbrehm.pdf

22. Ibid.

23. Open Letter from Stephen Reisner, Stephen Soldz, and Brad Olsen to APA president Sharon Brehm, June 21, 2007. http://psychoanalystsopposewar.org/blog/wp-content/uploads/2007/06/replytocolonellarryjames_3.pdf

24. Bloche and Marks.

25. Bill Morlin, "Expert Has Stake in Cryptic Local Firm; Consultants Tied to CIA Interrogations," *Spokesman-Review* (Spokane, WA), August 12, 2007.

26. *Democracy Now!,* September 28, 2007.

6. VOICES IN CONFLICT

1. Reprinted by permission of Charlie Anderson. www.charlese anderson.com
2. Original quote from *The Ground Truth*, a documentary film directed and produced by Patricia Foulkrod, 2006. www.groundtruth.net. Reprinted by permission of Focus Features.
3. Alison Leigh Cowan, "Play About Iraq War Divides Connecticut School," *New York Times*, March 24, 2007.
4. Barbara Alessi, "Setting the Record Straight on 'Voices,'" *Wilton Bulletin*, April 5, 2007.
5. Alison Leigh Cowan, "Play About Iraq War Divides Connecticut School," *New York Times*, March 24, 2007.
6. "Letters," *New York Times,* March 27, 2007. Reprinted by permission of the estate of Ira Levin.
7. Original quote from Brian Mockenhaupt, "I Miss Iraq. I Miss My Gun. I Miss My War." *Esquire*, March 2007. Reprinted by permission of Brian Mockenhaupt.
8. Reprinted by permission of Charlie Anderson. www.charleseanderson.com
9. Original quote from *The Ground Truth,* a documentary film directed and produced by Patricia Foulkrod, 2006. www.groundtruth.net. Reprinted by permission of Focus Features.
10. *Voices in Conflict*, directed by Bonnie Dickinson. Reprinted by permission of Bonnie Dickinson.
11. Ibid.

7. JUSTICE IN JENA

1. Howard Witt, "Supremacist Groups Seize on Jena 6 Dispute," *Chicago Tribune,* September 25, 2007.
2. Mark Potok, et al., "The Geography of Hate," *New York Times*, November 25, 2007.
3. Howard Witt, "Racial Demons Rear Heads," *Chicago Tribune,* May 20, 2007.
4. Darryl Fears, "La. Town Fells 'White Tree,' but Tensions Run Deep," *Washington Post*, August 4, 2007.
5. *Democracy Now!,* September 21, 2007.
6. "Fact Sheet—The School-to-Prison Pipeline in the National Context," ACLU. http://www.aclu.org/crimjustice/juv/24704res 20060321.html

7. *Arresting Development: Addressing the School Discipline Crisis in Florida,* NAACP Legal Defense Fund & Advancement Project, April 2006, p. 6. www.advancementproject.org/reports/Arstd Dvpm_SM.pdf

8. News Release, Advancement Project, April 20, 2006.

9. Howard Witt, "School Discipline Tougher on African Americans," *Chicago Tribune,* September 25, 2007.

10. "Fact Sheet—The School-to-Prison Pipeline in the National Context," ACLU.

11. *Education on Lockdown: The Schoolhouse to Jailhouse Track,* Advancement Project, March 24, 2005, pp. 7–8. www.advancement project.org/reports/FINALEOLrep.pdf

12. *Arresting Development,* p. 7.

13. Howard Witt, "School Discipline Tougher on African Americans," *Chicago Tribune*, September 25, 2007.

14. *Democracy Now!,* April 3, 2007.

15. *Arresting Development*, p. 6.

16. David Rohde and Christopher Drew, "Prisoners Evacuated After Hurricanes Allege Abuse," *New York Times,* October 2, 2005.

17. "Groundbreaking Held for LaSalle Detention Facility," *Jena Times,* September 2007.

18. Howard Witt, "Appeals Court Overturns Jena 6 Conviction," *Chicago Tribune,* September 14, 2007.

19. Mark Potok, et al., "The Geography of Hate," *New York Times*, November 25, 2007.

8. PEACE WARRIORS

1. "Military Personnel," Report GAO-07-1196, Government Accountability Office, September 2007.

2. Robert Hodierne, "Down on the War," *Military Times,* December 29, 2006.

3. Lolita Baldor, "Soldiers Going AWOL at High Rate," Associated Press, November 17, 2007.

4. Paul von Zielbauer, "U.S. Army Prosecutions of Desertion Rise Sharply," *International Herald Tribune,* April 8, 2007.

5. Marc Cooper, "About Face," *The Nation,* January 8, 2007; Andrew Bacevich, "Warrior Politics," *The Atlantic Monthly,* May 2007.

Index